Rick Steves®

POCKET

VIENNA

Rick Steves with Gene Openshaw

Contents

Introduction

Vienna is the capital of Austria, the cradle of classical music, and one of Europe's most livable cities. The city center is skyscraper free, pedestrian friendly, and traversed by electric trams. It retains a 19th-century elegance, when the city was at the forefront of the arts and sciences.

Today's Vienna—or Wien ("Veen")—is a modern city of 1.8 million people. With world-class museums and sights such as St. Stephen's Cathedral and the Hofburg Palace, there's plenty to keep a sightseer busy. But compared with most urban centers, the pace of life here is slow. People nurse a pastry and coffee over the daily news at small cafés. They sip wine under the stars, enjoy Mozart operas and Strauss waltzes, and continually work to perfect their knack for good living. Anyone with an interest in the arts, beautiful objects, or Sacher torte with whipped cream will feel right at home.

Vienna

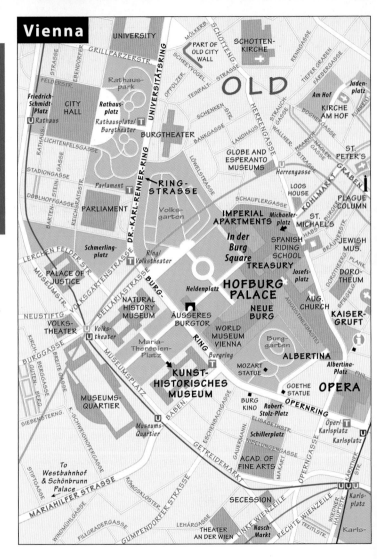

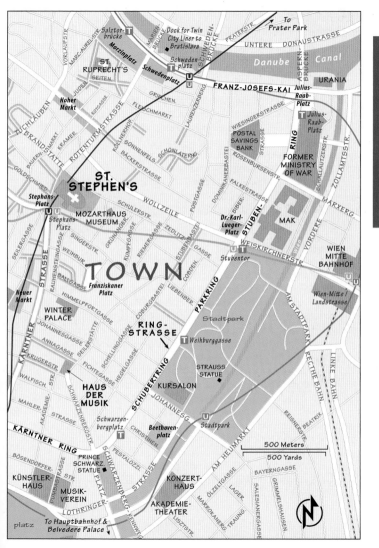

About This Book

Rick Steves Pocket Vienna is a personal tour guide...in your pocket. The core of the book is seven self-guided walks and tours that zero in on Vienna's greatest sights and experiences. The Vienna City Walk takes you through the heart of the city, while the Ringstrasse Tram Tour circles its elegant border. St. Stephen's Cathedral is a journey into Vienna's medieval past. At the Hofburg Palace, you're immersed in the Habsburg world—the opulent rooms of their Imperial Apartments and the crown jewels of the Treasury. The Kunsthistorisches Museum has some of the world's greatest paintings, from Titian to Rembrandt to Bruegel. Finally, there's a visit to Schönbrunn Palace, which combines beautiful art with the beauties of nature.

The rest of this book is a traveler's tool kit, with my best advice on how to save money, plan your time, use public transportation, and avoid lines at the busiest sights. You'll also get recommendations on hotels, restaurants, and activities.

Vienna by Neighborhood

Vienna lies nestled between the Vienna Woods and the Danube River. Picture the city map as a target: The bull's-eye is St. Stephen's Cathedral. Surrounding that is the old town, bound tightly by the circular road called the Ringstrasse. Farther out is another ring road, the Gürtel, that contains the rest of downtown. Outside that lies the uninteresting sprawl of modern Vienna. As big as Greater Vienna is, almost everything of interest to the traveler lies inside the Ring, near the Ring, or a short transit ride away.

Think of Vienna as a collection of neighborhoods:

Old Town (Within the Ring): Much of Vienna's sightseeing is located in this, the first district. Here you'll find St. Stephen's Cathedral, the Hofburg complex, the opera house, and many great shops and restaurants. St. Stephen's stands proudly in the center, at the intersection of the two main (pedestrian-only) streets: Kärntner Strasse and the Graben. To walk across the old town—say, from the opera house in the south to the Danube Canal in the north—takes about 30 minutes.

Ringstrasse: The ring road enclosing the old town is the former city wall. Now it's lined with grand buildings, such as the City Hall (Rathaus). Trams #1, #2, #71, #D, and #O travel along the Ring (which also has several stops for Vienna's subway—the U-Bahn), making the

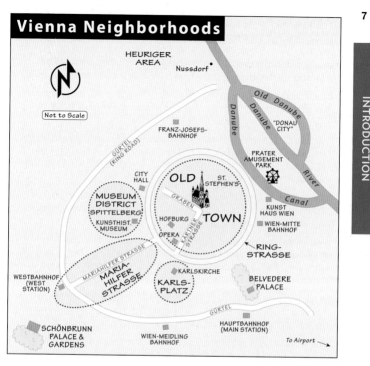

Vienna Neighborhoods

HEURIGER AREA

Nussdorf

Not to Scale

Old Danube

"DONAU CITY"

Danube

Danube

FRANZ-JOSEFS-BAHNHOF

GÜRTEL (RING ROAD)

CITY HALL

OLD

ST. STEPHEN'S

PRATER AMUSEMENT PARK

River

MUSEUM DISTRICT SPITTELBERG

GRABEN

TOWN

KUNST HAUS WIEN

Canal

KUNSTHIST. MUSEUM

HOFBURG

KÄRTNER STRASSE

WIEN-MITTE BAHNHOF

OPERA

RING-STRASSE

MARIAHILFER STRASSE

WESTBAHNHOF (WEST STATION)

MARIA-HILFER STRASSE

KARLSKIRCHE

KARLS-PLATZ

BELVEDERE PALACE

GÜRTEL

SCHÖNBRUNN PALACE & GARDENS

WIEN-MEIDLING BAHNHOF

HAUPTBAHNHOF (MAIN STATION)

To Airport

Ring a handy jumping-off point for sights located just inside or outside it.

Karlsplatz: The U-Bahn stop Karlsplatz (tram stop: Oper/Karlsplatz) is a major transportation hub on the Ring. Stretching south of here is a cluster of sights, including the Karlskirche (St. Charles' Church), Naschmarkt, and the Secession.

Museum District: Just west of the Ring lies this classy area with the Kunsthistorisches art museum and several lesser galleries (the MuseumsQuartier). The charming traffic-free neighborhood of Spittelberg is great for cafés and nightlife.

Mariahilfer Strasse: Stretching still farther southwest is this lively pedestrianized street running from the Ring to the Westbahnhof, linked by a string of convenient U-Bahn stops. This

Vienna at a Glance

▲▲▲**Hofburg Imperial Apartments** Lavish main residence of the Habsburgs. **Hours:** Daily 9:00-17:30, July-Aug until 18:00. See page 69.

▲▲▲**Hofburg Treasury** The Habsburgs' collection of jewels, crowns, and other valuables—the best on the Continent. **Hours:** Wed-Mon 9:00-17:30, closed Tue. See page 87.

▲▲▲**St. Stephen's Cathedral** Enormous, historic Gothic cathedral in the center of Vienna. **Hours:** Foyer and north aisle—daily 6:00-22:00; main nave—Mon-Sat 9:00-11:30 & 13:00-16:30, Sun 13:00-16:30, July-Aug until 17:30. See page 35.

▲▲▲**Vienna State Opera** Dazzling, world-famous opera house. **Hours:** By guided tour only; schedule varies, but more tours generally in the afternoon and in July-Aug. See page 132.

▲▲▲**Kunsthistorisches Museum** World-class exhibit of the Habsburgs' art collection, including works by Raphael, Titian, Caravaggio, Rembrandt, and Bruegel. **Hours:** Daily 10:00-18:00, Thu until 21:00, closed Mon Sept-May. See page 97.

▲▲▲**Schönbrunn Palace** Spectacular summer residence of the Habsburgs, rivaling the grandeur of Versailles. **Hours:** Daily 9:00-17:00, July-Aug until 17:30. See page 115.

▲▲**World Museum Vienna** Several collections, including armor, musical instruments, and ethnographic treasures in the elegant halls of a Habsburg palace. **Hours:** Thu-Mon 10:00-18:00, Tue until 21:00, closed Wed. See page 127.

▲▲**Albertina Museum** Habsburg residence with state apartments, world-class collection of graphic arts and modernist classics, and first-rate special exhibits. **Hours:** Daily 10:00-18:00, Wed and Fri until 21:00. See page 129.

▲▲**Kaisergruft** Crypt for the Habsburg royalty. **Hours:** Daily 10:00-18:00. See page 130.

▲▲**Haus der Musik** Modern museum with interactive exhibits on Vienna's favorite pastime. **Hours:** Daily 10:00-22:00. See page 132.

▲▲**Natural History Museum** Big, beautiful catalog of the natural world, featuring the ancient *Venus of Willendorf*. **Hours:** Thu-Mon 9:00-18:30, Wed until 21:00, closed Tue. See page 134.

▲▲**Belvedere Palace** Elegant palace of Prince Eugene of Savoy, with a collection of 19th- and 20th-century Austrian art (including Klimt). **Hours:** Daily 10:00-18:00. See page 139.

▲**Spanish Riding School** Prancing white Lipizzaner stallions. **Hours:** Performances nearly year-round (except Jan and mid-June-mid-Aug), usually Sat-Sun at 11:00, plus morning exercises generally Tue-Fri 10:00-11:00 (except July-mid-Aug). See page 127.

▲**St. Michael's Church Crypt** Final resting place of about 100 wealthy 18th-century Viennese. **Hours:** By tour only (usually in German), Fri-Sat, schedule varies. See page 131.

▲**St. Peter's Church** Beautiful Baroque church in the old center. **Hours:** Mon-Fri 8:00-19:00, Sat-Sun from 9:00. See page 133.

▲**Karlskirche** Baroque church offering the unique chance to ride an elevator up into the dome. **Hours:** Mon-Sat 9:00-18:00, Sun 11:00-19:00. See page 136.

▲**Academy of Fine Arts Painting Gallery** Small but exciting rotating art exhibits spanning centuries. **Hours:** Tue-Sun 10:00-18:00, closed Mon. See page 136.

▲**The Secession** Art Nouveau exterior and Klimt paintings in situ. **Hours:** Tue-Sun 10:00-18:00, closed Mon. See page 137.

▲**Naschmarkt** Sprawling, lively outdoor market. **Hours:** Mon-Fri 6:00-19:30, Sat until 18:00, closed Sun, closes earlier in winter. See page 138.

▲**Museum of Military History** Huge collection of artifacts tracing the military history of the Habsburg Empire. **Hours:** Daily 9:00-17:00. See page 141.

▲**Kunst Haus Wien** Modern art museum dedicated to zany local artist Hundertwasser. **Hours:** Daily 10:00-18:00. See page 142.

▲**Vienna Furniture Museum** Eclectic collection of Habsburg furniture. **Hours:** Tue-Sun 10:00-17:00, closed Mon. See page 142.

Greater Vienna has Prater Park...   ...and Schönbrunn, the royal summer palace.

vibrant corridor is filled with cafés, a small shopping mall, and many of my recommended (and best-value) hotels. The east end of the street is nicer—close to downtown and the Museum District. The west end near the train station is a little rough around the edges.

Greater Vienna: Though not a "neighborhood" at all, these widely scattered sights are nevertheless easily connected by public transit. You're less than 30 minutes away from the *Heuriger* wine gardens (to the north), Belvedere Palace (to the south), Prater amusement park (east), and Schönbrunn Palace (southwest).

Planning Your Time

The following day plans give an idea of how much an organized, motivated, and caffeinated person can see. Vienna is packed with sights and worth two days and two nights on even the speediest trip.

Day 1: Circle the Ringstrasse by tram, following my self-guided tour, which starts and ends at the opera house. Drop by the nearby TI for planning and ticket needs. Tour the Vienna State Opera. After lunch, follow my Vienna City Walk, including visits inside the Kaisergruft and St. Stephen's Cathedral. In the evening, go for dinner and a romantic stroll in the old center.

Day 2: Browse the colorful Naschmarkt. Tour the Kunst-historisches Museum. In the afternoon, tour the Hofburg's Imperial Apartments and Treasury. Enjoy a concert or opera, or visit a museum that's open late.

Day 3: Take an early U-Bahn out to Schönbrunn Palace (book timed-entry in advance). Afterward, visit the sights around Karlsplatz and the Belvedere Palace. In the evening, visit a *Heuriger* wine garden or enjoy another concert.

Rick's Free Audio Tours and Video Clips

Rick Steves Audio Europe, a free app, makes it easy to download my audio tours and listen to them offline as you travel. For this book (look for the 🎧), free audio tours cover my Vienna City Walk and my St. Stephen's Cathedral and Ringstrasse Tram tours. The app also offers my public radio show interviews with travel experts from around the globe. Scan the QR code on the inside front cover to find it in your app store, or visit RickSteves.com/AudioEurope.

Rick Steves Classroom Europe, a powerful tool for teachers, is also useful for travelers. This video library contains about 600 short clips excerpted from my public television series. Enjoy these videos as you sort through options for your trip and to better understand what you'll see in Europe. Check it out at Classroom.RickSteves.com.

With More Time: There's plenty more to choose from in Vienna. For suggestions, see the Sights and Activities chapters.

When to Go

Vienna's main tourist season runs roughly from May through September. Summer has many advantages: the best weather, very long days (light until after 21:00), and the busiest schedule of tourist fun. But crowds are a problem, and two Viennese institutions—the

Opera performances take the summer off...

...but guided tours are possible.

State Opera and Boys' Choir—don't perform in July and August. (The Lipizzaner stallions also take a break, from mid-June to mid-August.)

In spring and fall, travel tends to be less crowded and can be cheaper. The weather is decent but less predictable. In spring, a string of public holidays can limit sightseeing hours (but can also mean special festivities). In fall, wine festivals enliven the city, while forests and vineyards boast beautiful fiery colors.

Before You Go

You'll have a smoother trip if you tackle a few things ahead of time. For more details on these topics, see the Practicalities chapter and RickSteves.com, which has helpful travel-tip articles and videos.

Make sure your travel documents are valid. If your passport expires within six months of your return date, you need to renew it (allow 12-plus weeks). Be aware of entry requirements; you may need to register with the European Travel Information and Authorization System (ETIAS; quick and easy process, https://travel-europe.europa.eu/etias_en). Get passport and country-specific travel info at Travel.State.gov.

Arrange your transportation. Book your international flights. Figure out your transportation options. If traveling beyond Vienna, research train reservations, rail passes, and car rentals.

Book rooms well in advance, especially if your trip falls during peak season or any major holidays or festivals.

Reserve ahead for key sights. Major musical events can sell out far in advance. In summer, avoid long waits by reserving ahead (a day or two is enough) for Schönbrunn Palace. Planning ahead will guarantee you a seat to see the Lipizzaner stallions, Vienna Boys' Choir,

Stay at family-run hotels…

…and receive a warm welcome.

and performances at the Vienna State Opera—though I prefer cheap, on-the-spot experiences (such as same-day standing-room tickets for the opera).

Consider travel insurance. Compare the cost of insurance to the cost of your potential loss. Understand what protections your credit card might offer and whether your existing insurance (health, homeowners, or renters) covers you and your possessions overseas.

Manage your money. "Tap-to-pay" or "contactless" cards are widely accepted and simple to use. You may need your credit card's PIN for some purchases—request it if you don't have one. Alert your bank that you'll be using your cards in Europe. You don't need to bring euros; you can withdraw euros from ATMs in Europe.

Use your smartphone smartly. Sign up for an international service plan to reduce your costs, or rely on Wi-Fi in Europe instead. Download any apps you'll want on the road, such as maps, translators, and Rick Steves Audio Europe (see sidebar, earlier).

Pack light. You'll walk with your luggage more than you think. I travel for weeks with a single carry-on bag and a day pack. Use the packing checklist in Practicalities as a guide.

Travel Smart

If you have a positive attitude, equip yourself with good information (this book), and expect to travel smart, you will.

Pickpockets abound in crowded places where tourists congregate. Treat commotions as smokescreens for theft. Keep your passport and backup cash and cards secure in a money belt tucked under your clothes; carry only a day's spending money and a card in your front pocket or wallet.

If you wilt easily, choose a hotel with air-conditioning, start your day early, take a midday siesta, and resume your sightseeing later.

Be sure to schedule in slack time for picnics, laundry, people-watching, leisurely dinners, shopping, and recharging your touristic batteries. Slow down and be open to unexpected experiences and the hospitality of the Viennese people.

Nurse a coffee and pastry at a neighborhood *Kaffeehaus,* linger over a glass (or two) at a wine garden, or spend an elegant evening at the opera. As you visit places I know and love, I'm happy you'll be meeting some of my favorite Austrians.

Happy travels! *Gute Reise!*

Vienna City Walk

Vienna, one of Europe's grandest cities of the past, is also a vibrant city of today. On this walk, we'll lace together the city's three most important landmarks. We start at the opera house, ground zero for Vienna's international reputation for classical music. We'll make our way to St. Stephen's Cathedral, with its skyscraping spire, the symbol of the city. The walk ends at the Hofburg Palace—once the home of the Habsburgs, now brimming with top-notch museums.

Along the way, we'll drop into some smaller sights that help make this city so intriguing, and get immersed in the Vienna of today. It's a laid-back world of genteel shops, cafés, chocolate, and Sacher torte.

This walk is a first look at the city. Use it to get the lay of the land and an overview of sights to explore in depth later. It's a sampler of Vienna's best—past and present.

ORIENTATION

Length of This Walk: Allow one hour; more if you tour any major sights along the way.

When to Go: This walk works just as well in the evening as it does during the day, as long as you don't plan on touring some of the sights you'll pass.

Opera House: A visit is possible only with a guided tour (see page 132).

Albertina Museum: €19, daily 10:00-18:00, Wed and Fri until 21:00. Kaisergruft: €8, daily 10:00-18:00.

St. Stephen's Cathedral: Church foyer and north aisle—free, daily 6:00-22:00; main nave—€6, includes audioguide, Mon-Sat 9:00-11:30 & 13:00-16:30, Sun 13:00-16:30, July-Aug until 17:30. The cathedral's towers and catacombs have varying costs and hours— 📖 see the St. Stephen's Cathedral Tour chapter for specifics.

St. Peter's Church: Free; Mon-Fri 8:00-19:00, Sat-Sun from 9:00; free organ concerts daily at 15:00.

St. Michael's Church Crypt: €8 for mandatory 45-minute tour, tours run Fri-Sat only and may only be in German.

Hofburg Imperial Apartments: €16, covered by Sisi Ticket (see page 126), daily 9:00-17:30, July-Aug until 18:00, last entry one hour before closing.

Hofburg Treasury: €14, €24 combo-ticket with Kunsthistorisches Museum, Wed-Mon 9:00-17:30, closed Tue.

Tours: 🎧 Download my free Vienna City Walk audio tour. For efficiency, you can splice my St. Stephen's Cathedral audio tour (see next chapter) into this walk.

Starring: Vienna's "big three" (opera house, cathedral, palace), plus an array of sights, squares, and shops tucked between them.

THE WALK BEGINS

▶ *Begin at the square outside Vienna's landmark opera house, home of the Vienna State Opera.*

❶ Opera House

If Vienna is the world capital of classical music, this building is its throne room. It's typical of Vienna's 19th-century buildings in that it features a revival style—Neo-Renaissance—with arched windows, half-columns, and the sloping, copper mansard roof typical of French Renaissance *châteaux*.

Since the structure was built in 1869, almost all of the opera world's luminaries have passed through here. Its former musical directors include Gustav Mahler, Herbert von Karajan, and Richard Strauss. Luciano Pavarotti, Maria Callas, Placido Domingo, and many other greats have sung from its stage.

In the pavement along the side of the opera house (and all along Kärntner Strasse), you'll find plaques forming a Hollywood-style walk of fame. These represent the stars of classical music—famous composers, singers, musicians, and conductors. Look up at the building. During opera season, you'll notice the giant outdoor screen that shows some live performances (as noted in the posted schedules and on the screen itself).

If you're a fan, take a guided tour of the opera. Or consider an evening performance (standing-room tickets are surprisingly cheap; see the Activities chapter).

The opera house marks a busy intersection in Vienna, where Kärntner Strasse meets the Ring. The Karlsplatz U-Bahn station in

The opera house was built for royalty…   …but commoners enjoy the live video feed.

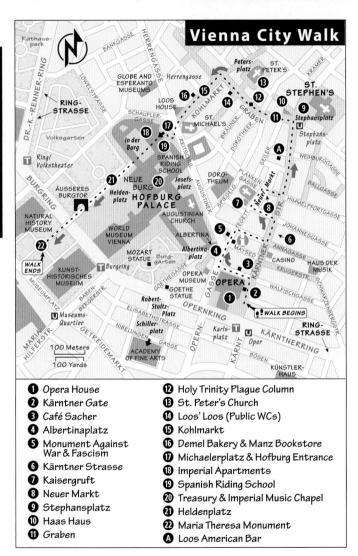

Vienna City Walk

1. Opera House
2. Kärntner Gate
3. Café Sacher
4. Albertinaplatz
5. Monument Against War & Fascism
6. Kärntner Strasse
7. Kaisergruft
8. Neuer Markt
9. Stephansplatz
10. Haas Haus
11. Graben
12. Holy Trinity Plague Column
13. St. Peter's Church
14. Loos' Loos (Public WCs)
15. Kohlmarkt
16. Demel Bakery & Manz Bookstore
17. Michaelerplatz & Hofburg Entrance
18. Imperial Apartments
19. Spanish Riding School
20. Treasury & Imperial Music Chapel
21. Heldenplatz
22. Maria Theresa Monument
A. Loos American Bar

front of the opera is an underground shopping mall with fast food, newsstands, and lots of pickpockets.

▶ *With your back to the Ringstrasse and the opera house on your left, face the busy pedestrian boulevard that leads into the center of town.*

❷ Kärntner Gate

Even though the center of town sits on an irregular medieval street plan, you'll notice the parallel rows of more modern, uniform buildings in front of you. These were built where the city wall once stood. The opera's lower stage is where the old moat used to be—outside the walls. This was a main gate, through which a road led to the Kärnten (Carinthia) region of southern Austria.

Notice the pedestrian signals and how they feature both gay and straight couples. Vienna's Green Party is part of the city's current ruling coalition and they like to remind the world that, while Austria's national government is more conservative (reflecting the fears and concerns of rural and small-town voters), Vienna celebrates diversity.

▶ *Walk behind the opera and across the street toward the dark-red awning to find the famous...*

❸ Café Sacher

This is the home of the world's classiest chocolate cake, the Sacher torte: two layers of cake separated by apricot jam and covered in dark-chocolate icing, usually served with whipped cream. It was invented in a fit of improvisation in 1832 by Franz Sacher, dessert chef to Prince Metternich (the mastermind diplomat who redrew the map of post-Napoleonic Europe). The cake became world famous when the inventor's son served it next door at his hotel (you may have noticed the fancy door attendants). Many locals complain that the cakes here have gone downhill, and some tourists are surprised by how dry they are—you really need that dollop of *Schlagobers*.

For a more genuine serving of 19th-century Viennese elegance, have your coffee and cake at the recommended **Gerstner Café** (facing the opera, back on Kärntner Strasse at #51). Enter under the green awnings, climb to the third level, and spend a little time back in the 1860s.

▶ *Continue past Hotel Sacher. On a corner (to the right) at the end of the street, the Vienna TI has a handy ticket desk for concerts. And dead*

Break time. Sacher torte, supposedly invented here, comes with whipped cream, or *Schlagobers*.

ahead is a small, triangular, cobbled square adorned with memorial sculptures.

❹ Albertinaplatz

Overlooking the square, the tan-and-white Neoclassical building marks the tip of the Hofburg Palace—the sprawling complex of buildings that was long the seat of Habsburg power. The balustraded terrace up top was the balcony of Empress Maria Theresa's daughter Maria Christina, who lived here. Today, her home houses the **Albertina Museum,** topped by a sleek, titanium canopy (called the "diving board" by critics). The museum's plush, 19th-century state rooms are the only Neoclassical (post-Rococo) palace rooms anywhere in the Habsburg realm. And the Batliner Collection of modernist paintings (Monet to Picasso) is a delight (see page 129).

Albertinaplatz itself is filled with sculptures that make up the powerful, thought-provoking ❺ **Monument Against War and Fascism,** which commemorates the dark years when Austria came under Nazi rule (1938-1945). The memorial has four parts. The split white monument, *The Gates of Violence,* remembers victims of all wars and violence. Standing directly in front of it, you're at the gates

Dive into art at the Albertina Museum.

A stark reminder of the Fascist years

of a concentration camp. Then, as you explore the statues, you step into a montage of wartime images: clubs and WWI gas masks, a dying woman birthing a future soldier, victims of cruel medical experimentation, and chained slave laborers sitting on a pedestal of granite cut from the infamous quarry at the former concentration camp at Mauthausen. The hunched-over figure on the ground behind is a Jew forced to scrub anti-Nazi graffiti off a street with a brush. Of Vienna's 200,000 Jews, more than 65,000 died in Nazi concentration camps. The sculpture with its head buried in the stone is Orpheus entering the underworld, meant to remind everyone of the victims of Nazism... and the consequences of not keeping our governments on track.

Viewing this monument gains even more emotional impact when you realize what happened on this spot: During a WWII bombing attack, several hundred people were buried alive when the cellar they were using as shelter was demolished.

Behind the monument is **Café Tirolerhof,** a classic Viennese café. Refreshingly air-conditioned, it's full of things that time has passed by: chandeliers, marble tables, upholstered booths, formally dressed servers, and newspapers. (For more on Vienna's cafés, see the Eating chapter.)

▶ *From the café, turn right on Führichsgasse. Walk one block until you hit...*

❻ Kärntner Strasse

This grand, traffic-free street is the people-watching delight of this in-love-with-life city. Today's Kärntner Strasse is mostly a crass commercial pedestrian mall—its famed elegant shops long gone. But locals

From the opera to the cathedral, Kärntner Strasse cuts through the center of Vienna.

know it's the same road Crusaders marched down as they headed off from St. Stephen's Cathedral for the Holy Land in the 12th century. Today it's full of shoppers.

As you walk, be sure to look up, above the modern storefronts, for glimpses of the street's former glory. On the left at #26: **J & L Lobmeyr Crystal** ("Founded in 1823") still has its impressive brown storefront with gold trim, statues, and the Habsburg double eagle. In the market for some $400 napkin rings? Lobmeyr's your place. Inside, breathe in the classic Old World ambience as you peruse the wares and visit the glass museum (free entry; ground floor—glasses and chandeliers, first floor—silver and Murano glass, second floor—museum; closed Sun).

▶ *At the end of the block, turn left on Marco d'Aviano Gasse (passing the fragrant flower stall) to make a short detour to the square called Neuer Markt. Straight ahead is an orange-ish church with a triangular roof and cross, the Capuchin Church. In its basement is the...*

❼ Kaisergruft

Under the church sits the Imperial Crypt, filled with what's left of Austria's emperors, empresses, and other Habsburg royalty. For centuries, Vienna was the heart of a vast empire ruled by the Habsburg family, and here is where they lie buried in their fancy pewter coffins. You'll find all the Habsburg greats, including Maria Theresa, her son Josef II (Mozart's patron), Franz Josef, and Empress Sisi. Before moving on, consider paying your respects here (see page 130).

▶ *Stretching north from the Kaisergruft is the square called...*

❽ Neuer Markt

In the center of Neuer Markt is the **four rivers fountain** showing Lady Providence surrounded by figures symbolizing the rivers that flow into the Danube. The sexy statues offended Empress Maria Theresa, who actually organized "Chastity Commissions" to defend her capital city's moral standards.

▶ *Return to Kärntner Strasse. As you approach St. Stephen's Cathedral, you're likely to first see it as a reflection in the round-glass windows of the postmodern Haas Haus. Pass the U-Bahn station (which has WCs) where the street spills into Vienna's main square...*

St. Stephen's glorious 700-year history...   ...is reflected in this modern building.

❾ Stephansplatz

The cathedral's frilly spire looms overhead, worshippers and tourists pour inside the church, and shoppers buzz around the outside. You're at the center of Vienna.

The Gothic **St. Stephen's Cathedral** (c. 1300-1450) is known for its 450-foot south tower; its colorful, patterned roof; and its place in Viennese history. When it was built, it was a huge church for what was then a small town, and it helped put the fledgling city on the map. At this point, you may want to take a break from this walk to tour the church (📖 see the St. Stephen's Cathedral Tour chapter or 🎧 download my audio tour).

Facing St. Stephen's is the sleek concrete-and-glass ❿ **Haas Haus,** a postmodern building by noted Austrian architect Hans Hollein (finished in 1990). The curved facade is supposed to echo the Roman fortress of Vindobona (its ruins were found near here). Notice how the smooth, rounded glass reflects St. Stephen's pointy architecture, providing a great photo opportunity—especially at twilight. The café and pricey restaurant on the rooftop offer a nice perch (take the elevator up to the sixth floor, and walk up one flight to reach the rooftop terrace and restaurant).

▶ *Exit the square with your back to the cathedral. Walk past the Haas Haus, and bear right down the street called the...*

⓫ Graben

This was once a *Graben,* or ditch—originally the moat for the Roman military camp. Back during Vienna's 19th-century heyday, more than 200,000 people were packed into the city's inner center (inside the

Ringstrasse), walking on dirt streets. Today this area houses 20,000. The Graben was a busy street with three lanes of traffic until the 1970s, when the city inaugurated its new subway system and the street was turned into one of Europe's first pedestrian-only zones. Take a moment to absorb the scene—you're standing in an area surrounded by history, postwar rebuilding, grand architecture, fine cafés, and people enjoying life...for me, quintessential Europe.

In another 50 yards, you reach Dorotheergasse, on your left, which leads (after two more long blocks) to the **Dorotheum** auction house. Consider poking your nose in here later for some fancy window shopping. Also along this street are two recommended eateries: the sandwich shop Trześniewski—one of my favorite places for lunch—and the classic Café Hawelka.

In the middle of the Graben pedestrian zone is the extravagantly blobby ⓬ **Holy Trinity plague column** (*Pestsäule*). The 60-foot pillar of clouds sprouts angels and cherubs, with the wonderfully gilded Father, Son, and Holy Ghost at the top (all protected by an anti-pigeon net).

In 1679, Vienna was hit by a massive epidemic of bubonic plague. Around 75,000 Viennese died—about a third of the city. Emperor Leopold I dropped to his knees (something emperors never did in public) and begged God to save the city. (Find Leopold about a quarter of the way up the monument, just above the brown banner. Hint: The typical inbreeding of royal families left him with a gaping underbite.) His prayer was heard by Lady Faith (the statue below Leopold, carrying a cross). With the help of a heartless little cupid, she tosses an old naked woman—symbolizing the plague—into the abyss and saves the city. In gratitude, Leopold vowed to erect this monument, which

Graben with its gold-tipped plague column

The emperor prays for Vienna to be saved.

Adolf Loos (1870-1933)

"Decoration is a crime," wrote Adolf Loos, the turn-of-the-20th-century architect who was Vienna's answer to Frank Lloyd Wright. He lived in a time when most buildings were plastered with fake Greek columns, frosted with Baroque balustrades, and studded with statues. But Loos—foreshadowing the Modernist style of "less is more" and "form follows function"— stripped buildings down to their structural skeletons.

On this walk, you'll pass several examples of his work. The **Loos American Bar** (a half-block off Kärntner Strasse, on the left just before Stephansplatz at Kärntner Durchgang 10) has a cubical facade, with square columns and crossbeams (and no flowery capitals). The interior is elegant and understated, with rich marble and mirrors that appear to expand the small space. As they have little patience with gawkers, the best way to admire the interior is to sit down and order a drink. Farther ahead are Loos' **public WCs** (on Graben), the cube-shaped **Manz Bookstore,** the boldly stripped-down **Loos House** (on Michaelerplatz), and the **Loos Room** in the Wien Museum Karlsplatz (www.wienmuseum.at).

became a model for cities throughout the empire that were ravaged by the same plague.

▶ *Thirty yards past the plague monument, look down the short street to the right, which frames a Baroque church with a stately green dome.*

⓭ St. Peter's Church

Leopold I ordered this church to be built as a thank-you for surviving the 1679 plague. The church stands on the site of a much older church that may have been Vienna's first (or second) Christian church. Inside, St. Peter's shows Vienna at its Baroque best (see page 133). Note that the church offers free organ concerts (daily at 15:00, advertised at the entry).

▶ *Continue west on the Graben, where you'll immediately find some stairs leading underground to…*

⑭ Loos' Loos

In about 1900, a local chemical maker needed a publicity stunt to prove that his chemicals really got things clean. He purchased two wine cellars under the Graben and had them turned into classy WCs in the Modernist style (designed by Adolf Loos—see sidebar), complete with chandeliers and finely crafted mahogany. While the chandeliers are gone, the restrooms remain a relatively appealing place to do your business. Locals and tourists happily pay €0.50 for a quick visit.

▶ *The Graben dead-ends at the aristocratic supermarket Julius Meinl am Graben. From here, you could turn right into Vienna's "golden corner," with the city's finest shops. But we'll turn left. In the distance is the big green-and-gold dome of the Hofburg, where we'll head soon. The street leading up to the Hofburg is…*

⑮ Kohlmarkt

This is Vienna's most elegant and unaffordable shopping street, lined with Cartier, Armani, Gucci, Tiffany, and the emperor's palace at the end. Strolling Kohlmarkt, daydream about ⑯ **Demel,** the ultimate Viennese chocolate shop (#14, daily 9:00-19:00). While people line up to enjoy their famous café, there's no wait to walk through the café to the shop in back, where you'll find a room filled with Art Nouveau boxes of Empress Sisi's choco-dreams come true: *Kandierte Veilchen* (candied violet petals), *Katzenzungen* (cats' tongues), and so on. The

Kohlmarkt, a high-end shopping street

Royals ate Demel's cakes—and so can you.

cakes here are moist (compared with the dry Sacher tortes). Shops like this boast "K.u.K."—signifying that during the Habsburgs' heyday, they were patronized by the *König und Kaiser* (king and emperor—same guy).

Next to Demel, the **Manz Bookstore** has a Loos-designed facade (see the "Adolf Loos" sidebar).

▶ *Kohlmarkt ends at the square called...*

⑰ Michaelerplatz

This square is dominated by the **Hofburg Palace.** Study the grand Neo-Baroque facade, dating from about 1900. The four heroic giants illustrate Hercules wrestling with his great challenges (Emperor Franz Josef, who commissioned the gate, felt he could relate).

In the center of this square, a scant bit of **Roman Vienna** lies exposed just beneath street level.

Michaelerplatz Spin Tour: Do a slow, clockwise pan to get your bearings, starting (over your left shoulder as you face the Hofburg) with **St. Michael's Church,** which offers fascinating tours of its crypt (see page 131). To the right of that is the fancy **Loden-Plankl shop,** with traditional Austrian formalwear, including dirndls. Farther to the right, across Augustinerstrasse, is the wing of the palace that houses the **Spanish Riding School** and its famous white Lipizzaner stallions. Farther down this street lies **Josefsplatz,** with the **Augustinian Church** (see page 128), and the Dorotheum auction house. At the end of the street are Albertinaplatz and the opera house (where we started this walk).

Continue your spin: Two buildings over from the Hofburg (to the right), the **Loos House** has a facade featuring a perfectly geometrical grid of square columns and windows. Compared to the Neo-Baroque facade of the Hofburg, the stern Modernism of the Loos House appears to be from an entirely different age. And yet, both of these—as well as the Eiffel Tower and Mad Ludwig's fairy-tale Neuschwanstein Castle—were built in the same generation, roughly around 1900. In many ways, this jarring juxtaposition exemplifies the architectural turmoil of the turn of the 20th century and represents the passing of the torch from Europe's age of divine monarchs to the modern era.

▶ *Let's take a look at where Austria's glorious history began—at the...*

Where New Faces Down Old

It's fascinating to think of Michaelerplatz as the architectural embodiment of a fundamental showdown that took place at the dawn of the 20th century, between the old and the new.

Emperor Franz Josef came to power during the popular revolution year of 1848 (as an 18-year-old, he was locked in his palace for safety). Once in power, he saw that the real threat to him was not from without, but from within. He dismantled the city wall and moved his army's barracks to the center of the city. But near the end of his reign, the modern world was clearly closing in.

Franz Josef's Neo-Baroque design for the Hofburg, featuring huge statues of Hercules in action at the gate, represents a desperate last stand of the absolutism of the emperor. Hercules was a favorite of emperors—a prototype of the modern ruler. The only mythical figure that was half-god, Hercules earned this half-divinity with hard labors. Like Hercules, the emperor's position was a combination of privileged birth and achievement—legitimized both by God and by his own hard work.

A few decades after Franz Josef erected his celebration of divine right, Loos responded with his starkly different building across the street. Although the Loos House might seem boring today, in its time, this anti-Historicist, anti-Art Nouveau statement was shocking. Inspired by his studies in the US (and by Frank Lloyd Wright), Loos designed what was Vienna's first "modern" building, with a trapezoidal footprint that makes no attempt to hide the awkwardly shaped street corner it stands on. Windows lack the customary cornice framing the top—a "house without eyebrows."

And so, from his front door, the emperor had to look at the modern world staring him rudely in the face, sneering, "Divine power is B.S. and your time is past." The emperor was angered by the bank building's lack of decor. Loos relented only slightly by putting up the 10 flower boxes (or "mustaches") beneath the windows.

But a few flowers couldn't disguise the notion that the divine monarchy was beginning to share Vienna with new ideas. As Loos worked, Stalin, Hitler, Trotsky, and Freud were all rattling about Vienna. Women were smoking and riding bikes. It was a scary time…a time ripe with change. And, of course, after the Great War, the Habsburgs and the rest of Europe's autocratic imperial families were history.

Hofburg Imperial Palace

This is the complex of palaces where the Habsburg emperors lived out their lives (except in summer, when they resided at Schönbrunn Palace). Enter the Hofburg through the gate, where you immediately find yourself beneath a big rotunda. The doorway on the right is the entrance to the ⓲ **Imperial Apartments,** where the Habsburg emperors once lived in chandeliered elegance. Today you can tour its lavish rooms, as well as a museum about Empress Sisi, and a porcelain and silver collection (📖 see the Hofburg Imperial Apartments Tour chapter). To the left is the ticket office for the ⓳ **Spanish Riding School.**

Continuing on, you emerge from the rotunda into the main courtyard of the Hofburg, called **In der Burg.** The Caesar-like statue is of Habsburg Emperor Franz II (1768-1835), grandson of Maria Theresa, grandfather of Franz Josef, and father-in-law of Napoleon. To the right of Franz are the Imperial Apartments, and to the left are the offices of Austria's mostly ceremonial president (the more powerful chancellor lives in a building just behind this courtyard).

Franz Josef faces the oldest part of the palace: a colorful red, black, and gold gateway. Through the gate lies the ⓴ **Treasury** (Schatzkammer; 📖 see the Hofburg Treasury Tour chapter) and the **Imperial Music Chapel** (Hofmusikkapelle; see page 155), where the Vienna Boys' Choir sings Mass. Ever since Joseph Haydn and Franz Schubert were choirboys here, visitors have gathered like groupies on Sundays to hear the famed choir sing.

Returning to the bigger In der Burg courtyard, face Franz and turn left, passing through the **tunnel,** with a few tourist shops and restaurants, to spill out into spacious ㉑ **Heldenplatz** (Heroes' Square).

Hofburg entrance in Neo-Rococo style

One of many courtyards in the vast palace

On the left is the impressive curved facade of the **World Museum Vienna** (formerly the New Palace). This vast wing was built in the early 1900s to be the new Habsburg living quarters and was meant to have a matching building facing it. But in 1914, the heir to the throne, Archduke Franz Ferdinand—while waiting politely for his long-lived uncle, Emperor Franz Josef, to die—was assassinated in Sarajevo. The archduke's death sparked World War I and the eventual end of eight centuries of Habsburg rule.

The World Museum Vienna contains an eclectic collection of ethnography, weaponry, suits of armor, musical instruments, and ancient Greek statues (see page 127). The two equestrian statues depict Prince Eugene of Savoy (1663-1736), who battled the Ottoman Turks, and Archduke Charles (1771-1847), who battled Napoleon.

Heldenplatz Spin Tour: Make a slow 360-degree turn, and imagine this huge square filled with people.

In 1938, 300,000 Viennese gathered here, entirely filling vast Heroes' Square, to welcome Adolf Hitler and celebrate their annexation with Germany—the *Anschluss*. The Nazi tyrant stood on

In Heldenplatz, a 20th-century extension of the Hofburg, a heroic statue gazes toward City Hall.

the balcony of the then New Palace and declared, "Before the face of German history, I declare my former homeland now a part of the Third Reich. One of the pearls of the Third Reich will be Vienna." He never said "Austria," a word that was now forbidden.

When pondering why the Austrians—eyes teary with joy and vigorously waving their Nazi flags—so willingly accepted Hitler's rule, it's important to remember that in 1938 Austria was already a fascist nation. The once vast and mighty empire of 50 million at its 19th-century peak came out of World War I a tiny landlocked land of six million that now suffered terrible unemployment. The opportunistic Hitler promised jobs along with a return to greatness—and the Austrian people gobbled it up.

Standing here, it's fascinating to consider Austrian aspirations for grandeur. In fact, the Habsburgs envisioned an ancient Rome-inspired Imperial Forum stretching from here across the Ringstrasse.

▶ *Walk on through the Greek-columned passageway (the Äusseres Burgtor), cross the Ringstrasse, and stand between the giant Kunsthistorisches and Natural History Museums, built in the 1880s to house the private art and scientific collections of the empire and to celebrate its culture and power. The emperor planned to tie these grand buildings and the palace together with two mighty triumphal arches spanning the Ringstrasse, connecting them into an awe-inspiring ensemble. While the emperor's vision died with his empire, a huge statue of the powerful empress Maria Theresa stands in the center of it all.*

㉒ Maria Theresa Monument

Vienna's biggest monument shows the empress (the empire's only female ruler) holding a scroll from her father granting the right of a woman to inherit his throne. Built in the 1870s, a hundred years after Maria Theresa's death, the statues and reliefs surrounding her speak volumes about her reign: Her four top generals sit on horseback while her four top advisers stand. Behind them, reliefs celebrate cultural leaders of her day, including little Wolfie Mozart with mentor "Papa" Joseph Haydn (with his hand on Mozart's shoulder, facing the Natural History Museum). The moral of this propaganda: that a strong military and a wise ruler are prerequisites for a thriving culture—attributes that characterized the 40-year rule of the woman who was perhaps Austria's greatest monarch.

Maria Theresa ruled Habsburg Austria for 40 years.

▶ *Our walk is finished. You're in the heart of Viennese sightseeing. Surrounding this square are some of the city's top museums. And the Hofburg Palace itself contains many of Vienna's best sights and museums. From the opera to the Hofburg, from chocolate to churches, from St. Stephen's to Sacher tortes—Vienna waits for you.*

St. Stephen's Cathedral Tour

This massive church is the Gothic needle around which Vienna spins. According to the medieval vision of its creators, it stands like a giant jeweled reliquary, offering praise to God from the center of the city. The church and its towers, especially the 450-foot south tower, give the city its most iconic image. (Check your pockets for €0.10 coins; those minted in Austria feature the south tower.) The cathedral has survived Vienna's many wars and today symbolizes the city's spirit and love of freedom.

The church has several worthwhile sights—some free, some requiring admission. On this tour, we'll pay to see the interior's main sights, and point out others you can see on your own.

The tower the locals call Steffl ("Stevie") still dominates the city as it did in this 17th-century drawing.

ORIENTATION

Cost: It's free to enter the foyer and north aisle of the church, but it costs €6 to get into the main nave, where most of the interesting items are located. The south and north towers and catacombs cost extra. The €20 combo-ticket covers everything but is overkill for most visitors.

Hours: The church doors are open daily 6:00-22:00, but the main nave is open for tourists Mon-Sat 9:00-11:30 & 13:00-16:30, Sun 13:00-16:30, July-Aug until 17:30. During services, when the main nave is reserved for worshippers, you can look into the church from the back.

Information: +43 1 515 523 054, www.stephanskirche.at.

Tours: Entry fee includes audioguide. 🎧 Or download my free St. Stephen's Cathedral audio tour.

Catacombs: The catacombs are open to the public only by guided tour (€6, daily 10:00-11:30 & 13:30-16:30, tours generally depart on the half-hour and are in German and English together). Just be at the stairs in the left/north transept to meet the guide—you'll pay at the end.

Towers: The iconic **south tower** rewards a tough climb up a claustrophobic, 343-step staircase with dizzying views (reach it via the entrance outside the church, around the right as you face the west facade; €5.50, daily 9:00-17:30). The shorter **north tower** holds the famous "Pummerin" bell, and you ascend via elevator (no stairs). While not as high as the south tower, the views are still great (€6, daily 9:00-20:30, entrance inside the church on the left/north side of the nave).

English Mass: Each Saturday at 19:00.

Theft Alert: It's a favorite for pickpockets. Be on guard.

Starring: The cathedral's mighty exterior and evocative interior, including an ornately carved pulpit and various bits and pieces of Austrian history.

St. Stephen's Cathedral

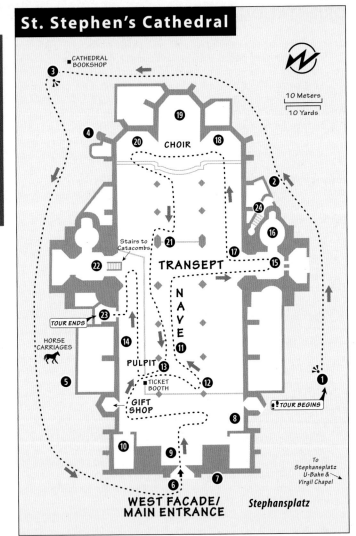

CATHEDRAL BOOKSHOP

10 Meters
10 Yards

CHOIR

Stairs to Catacombs

TRANSEPT

NAVE

TOUR ENDS

HORSE CARRIAGES

PULPIT

TICKET BOOTH

GIFT SHOP

TOUR BEGINS

To Stephansplatz U-Bahn & Virgil Chapel

WEST FACADE/ MAIN ENTRANCE

Stephansplatz

St. Stephen's Cathedral

❶ South Side View & Old Photos
❷ Reliefs, Memorials & Former Tombstones
❸ North Tower View
❹ Pulpit with Vanquished Turk
❺ Stonemason's Hut
❻ West Facade & Main Entrance
❼ 05 Sign
❽ Maria Pócs Icon
❾ Organ
❿ Chapel of Prince Eugene of Savoy
⓫ Main Nave
⓬ Pillar Statues (Madonna with the Protective Mantle)

⓭ Pulpit with Self-Portrait
⓮ Similar Self-Portrait
⓯ Mozart Plaque
⓰ Baptistery
⓱ Madonna of the Servants
⓲ Tomb of Frederick III
⓳ High Altar
⓴ Wiener Neustädter Altar
㉑ Plaque of Rebuilding
㉒ Catacombs Entry
㉓ North Tower (Elevator)
㉔ South Tower (Stairs)

THE TOUR BEGINS

Cathedral Exterior

Before we go inside, let's circle around the cathedral for a look at its impressive exterior. We'll stop at several points along the way to take it all in.

▶ As you face the church's main entry, go to the right across the little square. From here, you can absorb the sheer magnitude of this massive church, with its skyscraping spire.

❶ South Side

The church we see today is the third one on this spot. Today's church dates mainly from 1300 to 1450, when builders expanded on an earlier structure and added two huge towers at the end of each transept. When it was built, St. Stephen's—covering almost an acre of land—was a huge church for what was then just a modest town of 10,000. The ruler who built the church was competing with St. Vitus Cathedral, which was being built at the same time in Prague; he made sure that Vienna's grand church was bigger than Prague's. This helped convince the region's religious authorities that Vienna deserved a bishop, thus making St. Stephen's a "cathedral." Politically, this helped Vienna

WWII bomb damage has been lovingly repaired.

Habsburg eagles roost on the tiled roof.

become a city to be reckoned with, and it soon replaced Prague as the seat of the Holy Roman Empire.

The impressive 450-foot **south tower**—capped with a golden orb and cross—took 65 years to build and was finished in 1433. The tower is a rarity among medieval churches in that it was completed before the Gothic style—and the age of faith—petered out.

Find the Turkish **cannonball** stuck in a buttress (above the low, green roof on the middle buttress, marked with the date *1683*)—a souvenir from one of several Ottoman sieges of the city.

The nave's sharply pitched **roof** stands 200 feet tall and is covered in 230,000 colorful ceramic tiles. The zigzag pattern is purely decorative, with no special symbolism.

The cathedral was heavily damaged at the end of World War II. (Near where you are standing, at the base of the tower, there may be **old photos** showing the destruction.) In 1945, Vienna was caught in the chaos between the occupying Nazis and the approaching Soviets. Allied bombs sparked fires in nearby buildings, and the embers leapt to the cathedral rooftop. The original timbered Gothic roof burned, the cathedral's huge bell crashed to the ground, and the fire raged for two days. Civic pride prompted a financial outpouring, and the roof was rebuilt to its original splendor by 1952—doubly impressive considering the bombed-out state of the impoverished country at that time. Locals who contributed to the postwar reconstruction each had a chance to "own" one tile for their donation.

The little buildings lining the church exterior are **sacristies** (utility buildings used for running the church).

▶ Circle the church exterior counterclockwise, passing the **entrance to** *__the south tower__ (the 343-step tower climb is described at the end of this chapter).*

Just past the tower entrance, look for the carved ❷ **reliefs and memorials** and former **tombstones** now decorating the church wall. These are a reminder that the area around the church was a graveyard until the 18th century when it was cleaned out for health concerns.

▶ *As you hook around behind the church, pause at the cathedral bookshop (Dombuchhandlung) at the far corner of the square.*

❸ North Tower View

This spot provides a fine, wide-angle view of the stubby north tower and the apse of the church. From this vantage point, you can see the exoskeletal fundamentals of **Gothic architecture:** buttresses shoring up a very heavy roof, allowing for large windows that could be filled with stained glass to bathe the interior in colorful light. A battalion of storm-drain gargoyles stands ready to vomit water during downpours. Colored tiles on the roof show not the two-headed eagle of Habsburg times (as on the other side), but two distinct eagles of modern times

The dome-capped north tower is smaller but has the big bell that rings in Austria's New Year.

(1950): the state of Austria on the left and the city of Vienna on the right.

Just above street level, notice the marble ❹ **pulpit** under the golden starburst. Political ranting against other religions was only allowed outside the church. So, the priest would stand here, stoking public opinion against the Muslim Ottomans (or Jews or Protestants), in front of crowds far bigger than could fit into the church. Above the pulpit (in a scene from around 1700), a saint stands victoriously atop a vanquished Turk.

▶ *Continue circling the church, passing a line of horse carriages waiting to take tourists for a ride. Watch for the blocky, modern-looking building huddled next to the side of the cathedral. This is the...*

❺ Stonemason's Hut

There's always been a stonemason's hut here, as workers must keep the church in good repair. Even today, the masonry is maintained in the traditional way—a never-ending task. Unfortunately, the local limestone used in the Middle Ages is quite porous and absorbs modern pollution. Until the 1960s, this was a very busy traffic circle, and today's acidic air still takes its toll. Each winter, when rainwater soaks into the surface and then freezes, the stone corrodes—and must be repaired. Your church entry ticket helps fund this ongoing work.

Across the street (past the horse carriages) is the **archbishop's palace,** where the head of this church still lives today (enjoying a very short commute).

▶ *Around the corner is the cathedral's front door. Stand at the back of the square, across from the main entrance, to take in the entire...*

❻ West Facade

The Romanesque-style main entrance includes bits of the oldest part of the church (which stood here in the 1200s). Right behind you is the site of Vindobona, a Roman garrison town. Before the Romans converted to Christianity, there was a pagan temple here, and this entrance pays homage to that ancient heritage. Roman-era statues are embedded inside the facade, and the two **octagonal towers** flanking the main doorway are dubbed the "heathen towers" because they're built with a few recycled Roman stones (flipped over to hide the pagan inscriptions and expose the smooth sides).

Horse carriages cluster at the cathedral.

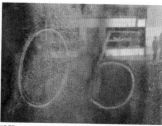

"O5"—symbol of anti-Nazi resistance

Ten yards to the right of the main doorway, about chest high, is the symbol ➐ **"O5,"** carved into the wall by anti-Nazi rebels (behind the Plexiglas, under the first plaque). The story goes that Hitler—who grew up in Austria—spurned his roots. When he attained power, he refused to call the country "Österreich," its native name, insisting on the Nazi term "Ostmark." Austrian patriots wrote the code "O5" to keep the true name alive: The "5" stands for the fifth letter of the alphabet (E), which often stands in for an umlaut, giving the "O" its correct pronunciation for "Österreich."

Step up to the main door. Before entering, study the details overhead. Christ—looking down from the tympanum—is triumphant over death. Flanked by angels with dramatic wings, he welcomes all. Ornate, tree-like pillars support a canopy of foliage and creatures, all full of meaning to the faithful medieval worshipper. The fine circa-1240 carvings above the door were once brightly painted. The paint was scrubbed off in the 19th century, when pure stone was more in vogue.

▶ *Enter the church.*

Cathedral Foyer

Find a spot to peer through the gate down the immense nave—more than a football field long and nine stories tall. It's lined with clusters of slender pillars that soar upward to support the ribbed crisscross arches of the ceiling. Stylistically, the nave is Gothic with a Baroque overlay. It's a spacious, glorious venue that's often used for high-profile concerts; check the "Concerts" page at StephansKirche.at to see what's on. We'll venture down the main nave soon, but first, take some time to explore the foyer area.

To the right as you enter, in a gold-and-silver sunburst frame, is a crude Byzantine-style ❽ **Maria Pócs Icon** (Pötscher Madonna), brought here from a humble Hungarian village church. The picture of Mary and Child is said to have wept real tears in 1697, as Central Europe was once again being threatened by the Turks. Prince Eugene of Savoy (described below) saved the day at the stunning Battle of Zenta in modern-day Serbia—a victory that broke the back of the Ottoman army. If you see crowds of pilgrims leaving flowers or lighting candles around the icon, they're most likely Hungarians thanking the Virgin for helping Prince Eugene drive the Ottomans out of their homeland.

Over the main doorway is the choir loft, with the 12,000-pipe ❾ **organ,** a 1960 replacement for the famous one destroyed during World War II. This organ, among Europe's biggest, was recently restored after being silent for 25 years.

Along the left wall is the **gift shop.** Step in to marvel at the 14th-century statuary decorating its wall—some of the finest carvings in the church.

To the left of the gift shop is the gated entrance to the ❿ **Chapel of Prince Eugene of Savoy.** Prince Eugene (1663-1736), a seminary student from France, arrived in Vienna in 1683 as the city was about to be overrun by the Ottoman Turks. He volunteered for the army and helped save the city, launching a brilliant career as a military man for the Habsburgs. His specialty was conquering the Ottomans. When he died, the grateful Austrians buried him here, under this chapel, marked by a tomb hatch in the floor.

▶ *Nearby is the entrance to the* ⓫ *main nave. Buy a ticket and walk to the center.*

Main Nave

▶ *Looking down the nave, note the statues on the columns (about 30 feet above the ground).*

⓬ Pillar Statues

The nave's columns are richly populated with 77 life-size stone statues, making a saintly parade to the high altar.

The nave—a football field long and nine stories tall—has massive pillars sporting 77 statues.

Check out the first pillar on the right (directly above the black metal fence). Facing the wall is the **Madonna with the Protective Mantle,** shown giving refuge to people of all walks of life (notice the many happy people of faith tucked under her cape). Also on that same pillar, find Moses with the Ten Commandments (to the left of the Madonna). On other columns, Bible students can find their favorite characters and saints—more Madonnas, St. George (killing the dragon), St. Francis of Assisi, arrow-pierced St. Sebastian, and so on.

▶ *Start down the nave toward the altar. At the second pillar on the left is the...*

⓭ Pulpit

The Gothic sandstone pulpit (c. 1500) is a masterpiece carved from three separate blocks (see if you can find the seams). A spiral stairway winds up to the lectern, surrounded and supported by the four "Latin Church Fathers," who translated the Bible into Latin in the fourth century (making it more widely accessible to the faithful) and whose writings influenced early Catholic dogma. Each has a very different

The ornate sandstone pulpit features the four church fathers. (That's Jerome in the hat.)

and very human facial expression (from back to front): Ambrose (day-dreamer), Jerome (skeptic), Gregory (explainer), and Augustine (listener).

The pulpit is as crammed with religious meaning as it is with beautifully realistic carvings. The top of the stairway's railing swarms with lizards and toads—symbols of corrupt teaching. The "Dog of the Lord" stands at the top, making sure none of those toads pollutes the sermon. Below the toads, wheels with three parts (the Trinity) roll up, while wheels with four spokes (the four seasons and four cardinal directions, symbolizing mortal life on earth) roll down.

Find the guy peeking out from under the stairs. This may be a **self-portrait of the sculptor.** In medieval times, art was done for the glory of God, and artists worked anonymously. But this pulpit was carved as humanist Renaissance ideals were creeping in from Italy—and individual artists were becoming famous. So, the artist included what may be a rare self-portrait bust in his work. He leans out from a window, sculptor's compass in hand, to observe the world and his work. The artist, long thought to be Hungarian mason Anton Pilgram, is now believed to be the Dutch sculptor Nicolaes Gerhaert van Leyden; both worked extensively on the cathedral.

About 20 paces toward the front, peering out from the left wall (about 15 feet up), is a similar ⓮ **self-portrait of the architect in color.** He holds a compass and L-square and symbolically shoulders the heavy burden of being a master builder of this huge place.

▶ *Continue up the nave. We'll visit several sights at the front of the church, moving in a roughly counterclockwise direction.*

Halfway up the nave, turn right and enter the south transept. Go all the way to the doors, then look left to find the...

Even the pulpit's staircase is symbolic.

The architect is depicted nearby.

Mozart in St. Stephen's Cathedral

Wolfgang Amadeus Mozart (1756-1791) was married in St. Stephen's, attended Mass here, and had two of his children baptized here.

Mozart spent most of his brief adult life in Vienna. Born in Salzburg, Mozart was a child prodigy who toured Europe. He performed for Empress Maria Theresa's family in Vienna when he was eight. At 25, he left Salzburg in a huff (freeing himself from his domineering father) and settled in Vienna. Here he found instant fame as a concert pianist and freelance composer, writing *The Marriage of Figaro, Don Giovanni, and The Magic Flute*. He married Constanze Weber in St. Stephen's, and they set up house in a lavish apartment a block east of the church (now the lackluster Mozarthaus museum—see page 133). Mozart lived at the heart of Viennese society—among musicians, actors, and aristocrats. He played in a string quartet with Joseph Haydn. Mozart may have heard Haydn playing the pipe organ right here.

After his early success, Mozart fell on hard times and the couple had to move to the suburbs. When Mozart died at 35, he was not buried at St. Stephen's, because the cemetery that once surrounded the church had been cleared out a decade earlier as an anti-plague measure. Instead, his remains were dumped into a mass grave outside town. But he was honored with a funeral service here in St. Stephen's.

⓯ Mozart Plaque

A plaque on the wall honors one of Vienna's most famous citizens—Wolfgang Amadeus Mozart, who had strong ties to this cathedral (see sidebar).

Look into the adjacent chapel at the fine ⓰ **baptistery** (stone bottom, matching carved-wood top, from around 1500). This is where Mozart's children were baptized.

On the right-hand column near the entrance to the south transept, notice the fine carved black stone statue of the **⑰ Madonna of the Servants** (from 1330). This remains a favorite of working people.

▶ *Now walk down the right aisle to the front. Dominating the chapel at the front-right corner of the church is the...*

⑱ Tomb of Frederick III

This imposing, red-marble tomb is like a big king-size-bed coffin with an effigy of Frederick lying on top (not visible—but there's a photo of the effigy on the left). The top of the tomb is decorated with his coats of arms, representing the many territories he ruled over. It's by the same Nicolaes Gerhaert van Leyden who likely sculpted the pulpit.

Frederick III (1415-1493) is considered the "father" of Vienna for turning the small village into a royal city with a cosmopolitan feel. Frederick secured a bishopric, turning the newly completed St. Stephen's church into a cathedral. The emperor's major contribution to Austria, however, was in fathering Maximilian I and marrying him off to Mary of Burgundy, instantly making the Habsburg Empire a major player in European politics. This lavish tomb (made of marble from Salzburg) is as long-lasting as Frederick's legacy. To make sure it stayed that way, locals saved his tomb from damage during World War II by encasing it in a shell of brick.

▶ *Walk to the middle of the church and face the...*

⑲ High Altar

The tall, ornate, black marble altarpiece (1641, by Tobias and Johann Pock) is topped with a statue of Mary that barely fits under the towering vaults of the ceiling. It frames a large painting of the stoning of St. Stephen, painted on copper. Stephen (at the bottom), having refused

Tomb of Frederick III, Vienna's patron...

...who commissioned this altarpiece

to stop professing his faith, is pelted with rocks by angry pagans. As he kneels, ready to die, he gazes up to see a vision of Christ, the cross, and the angels of heaven. The stained glass behind the painting—some of the oldest in the church—creates a kaleidoscopic jeweled backdrop.

Turn 180 degrees and look back for a view of the nave (not cluttered by the many Baroque chapels added in the 17th and 18th centuries, which are hidden behind the columns from this angle). What you see here is pretty close to a pure Gothic aesthetic.

▶ *Ten steps to the left of the main altar is the...*

⑳ Wiener Neustädter Altar

The triptych altarpiece—the symmetrical counterpart of Frederick III's tomb—was commissioned by Frederick in 1447. Its gilded wooden statues are especially impressive.

▶ *Return to the high altar and walk back up the middle of the nave. When you reach the third set of pillars, look immediately to the right (on the column with the black gate attached). About 10 feet above the ground is the...*

㉑ Plaque of Rebuilding

St. Stephen's is proud to be Austria's national church. The plaque explains in German how each region contributed to the rebuilding after World War II: *Die Glocke* (the bell) was financed by the state of Upper Austria. *Das Tor* (the entrance portal) was from Steiermark, the windows from Tirol, the pews from Vorarlberg, the floor from Lower Austria, and so on.

During World War II, many of the city's top art treasures were stowed safely in cellars and salt mines—hidden by both the Nazi occupiers (to protect against war damage) and by citizens (to protect against Nazi looters). The stained-glass windows behind the high altar were meticulously dismantled and packed away. The pulpit was encased, like the tomb of Frederick III, in a shell of brick. As the war was drawing to a close, it appeared St. Stephen's would escape major damage. But as the Nazis were fleeing, the bitter Nazi commander in charge of the city ordered that the church be destroyed. Fortunately, his underlings disobeyed. Unfortunately, the church accidentally caught fire during Allied bombing shortly thereafter, and the wooden roof collapsed onto the stone vaults of the ceiling. The

Tupperware-colored glass on either side of the nave dates from the 1950s.

From this spot consider the history St. Stephen's Cathedral has seen—and survived—as the towering centerpiece of this grand European capital.

▶ *Head back toward the main entrance. Along the north side of the nave, you have two options: Tour the catacombs or ascend the north tower (both described below). Or you can head outside for the pulse-raising climb up the south tower.*

Other Cathedral Sights

▶ *Near the middle of the church, at the left/north transept, is the entrance to the...*

㉒ Catacombs

The catacombs (viewable by guided tour only) hold the bodies—or at least the innards—of 72 Habsburgs, including that of Rudolf IV, the man who began building the south tower. This is where Austria's rulers were buried before the Kaisergruft was built (described in the Sights chapter), and where later Habsburgs' entrails were entombed. The copper urns preserve the imperial organs in alcohol. I touched Maria Theresa's urn and it wobbled.

▶ *Also in the north nave, but closer to the cathedral's main door, is the entrance for the north tower (look for the* Aufzug zur Pummerin *sign).*

㉓ North Tower

The cramped north tower elevator takes you to a fine (and sweat-free) view of the colorful cathedral rooftop, the city, and the Vienna Woods (which mark the start of a little mountain range called the Alps). And you get a close look at a very big bell. Nicknamed "the Boomer" (Pummerin), it's old (first cast in 1711), big (nearly 10 feet across), and very heavy (21 tons). By comparison, the Liberty Bell is four feet across and weighs one ton. The Pummerin was cast from cannons (and cannonballs) captured from the Ottomans when the siege of Vienna was lifted. These days, locals know the Pummerin as the bell that rings in the Austrian New Year.

▶ *Exit the church. Make a U-turn to the left if you're up for a climb up the...*

Finish your tour by climbing the south tower for views across the city to the Vienna Woods.

🎯 South Tower

The 450-foot-high south tower, once key to the city's defense as a look-out point, is still dear to Viennese hearts. (It's long been affectionately nicknamed "Steffl," Viennese for "Stevie.") No church spire in what was the Austro-Hungarian Empire is taller—by Habsburg decree. It offers a far better view than the north tower, but you'll earn it by hiking 343 tightly wound steps up the spiral staircase (burning about one Sacher torte's worth of calories). From the top, use your city map to locate the famous sights. There are great views of the colorful church roof, the low-level Viennese skyline (major skyscrapers are regulated in the city center), and—in the distance—the Vienna Woods.

▶ *Your tour is over. You're at the very center of Vienna.*

Ringstrasse Tram Tour

One of Europe's great streets, the Ringstrasse is lined with many of Vienna's top sights. In the 1860s, Emperor Franz Josef had Vienna's ingrown medieval wall torn down and replaced with a boulevard 190 feet wide. Vienna's grand "ring road," arcing nearly three miles around the city's core, predates all the buildings that line it.

This self-guided tram tour (a big circle starting and finishing at the opera house) gives you a good orientation and a ridiculously quick glimpse of some major sights as you glide by on Vienna's red trams (a.k.a. streetcars). No one tram makes the entire loop around the Ring, but you can see it all by transferring from tram #2 to tram #1 (at the Schwedenplatz stop). Enjoying this circular tram ride is a fun way to sit shoulder-to-shoulder with ordinary *Wieners* and see their city. In fact, my hope is that you'll feel like a *Wiener* yourself as you make this big loop.

PLANNING YOUR TOUR

This tour can be tricky to follow. To prepare, read and remember these pointers:

- You'll start the tour by boarding tram #2 directly across the busy street from the grand opera house. Buy your tram ticket before you board (there's a machine in the Opera U-Bahn station underpass). You'll be circling the city counterclockwise. Facing the opera house, you'll be heading to the right.

- Boarding a tram for this self-guided tour is like jumping onto a quickly moving sidewalk. Don't board until you are good and ready. Try to get a seat on the right-hand side for the first half of the ride (tram #2) and the left-hand side for the second half, on tram #1.

- Each numbered stop on this tour is named for and keyed to a tram stop. Each stop has a name that is announced in German as you approach and labeled in three places: usually in small print atop a round sign on the platform (only visible from the right-hand side); on monitors inside more modern trams; and on the map for this tour in your guidebook.

- When you reach each numbered stop, start reading the corresponding section (while the tram is loading). Finish reading it even if the tram pulls out. That way, you'll know what to look for once the tram rolls onward. Then enjoy the ride.

- Anyone following this tour must disembark at Schwedenplatz to change trams. But if you have a transit pass (instead of a ticket), you can—and should—jump on and off at other stops, seeing sights that interest you.

- Trams come every five or 10 minutes. The entire circle takes about a half-hour. Heck, you can even circle twice on the same ticket if you like.

The Oper stop, where we catch our tram

Our Ringstrasse tour uses trams #1 and #2.

ORIENTATION

Cost: €2.40 (one transit ticket). A single ticket can be used to cover the whole route, including the transfer between trams (but you're not otherwise allowed to interrupt your trip). However, with a transit pass (€8/24 hours), you're free to hop off and on. For more on riding Vienna's trams, see the Practicalities chapter.

When to Go: While this tour works fine in the daylight, the tram ride is also pleasant after dark, when nearly every sight on the route is well-lit and the tram is likely to be much less crowded.

Tours: ∩ Download my free Ringstrasse Tram Tour audio tour.

Length of This Tour: About 30-45 minutes; budget more time if you want to hop off and on along the way. Or consider making the loop a second time to just enjoy the ride and the many sights.

Bike Option: To do this approximately 3.25-mile tour at your own pace, you could rent a bike (see page 192). This allows you to easily stop at sights or to detour to nearby points of interest. The grassy median strip has excellent bike paths that run along almost the entire circuit of the Ring (except for a few blocks after the votive church, near the end of this tour).

Starring: Vienna's grandest boulevard, major landmarks, and a dizzyingly quick, once-over-lightly look at the city.

THE TOUR BEGINS

This tour makes a full circle around the ring road, with one transfer. You'll catch tram #2 from the middle of the street directly in front of the opera house and ride it for sections 1 through 5 of my tour. At Schwedenplatz (sections 6 and 7), you'll get out for a look at the Danube Canal before boarding tram #1 for sections 8 through 16. You'll end up exactly where you started—immediately across from the opera house.

When you're ready to start, hop on tram #2 going to the right, as you face the opera house; try to grab a seat on the right.

❶ Oper/Karlsplatz

Just past the opera house, look left and see the city's main pedestrian drag, Kärntner Strasse, leading to the zigzag-mosaic roof of **St. Stephen's Cathedral.** This tram tour makes a 360-degree circle

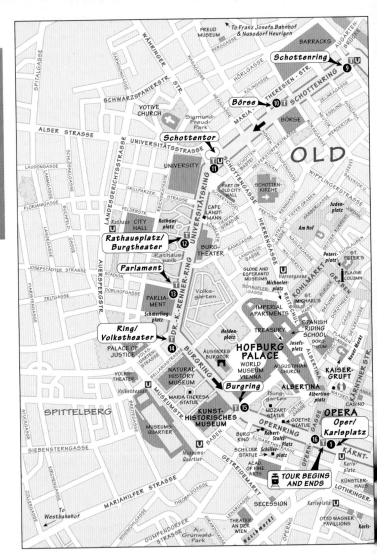

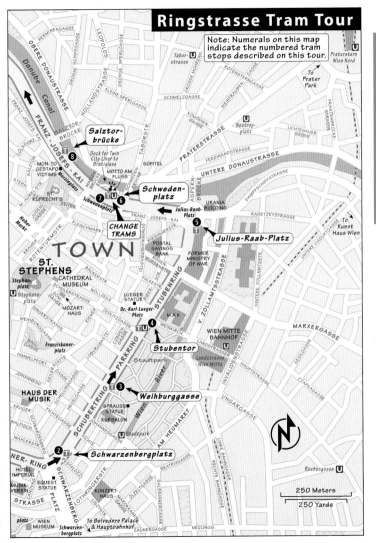

Note: Numerals on this map indicate the numbered tram stops described on this tour.

around the cathedral, staying about this same distance from the great church that marks the center of Vienna.

Along this stretch, you'll pass a string of Vienna's finest five-star hotels, including **Hotel Imperial** (after a couple blocks, on the right)—the choice of nearly every visiting big shot, from royalty to the Rolling Stones.

Fifty yards after the Hotel Imperial (just after the corner, also on the right), at Schwarzenbergplatz, an **equestrian statue** honors Prince Charles Schwarzenberg, who fought Napoleon. From the end of World War II until 1955, Austria and its capital were occupied by foreign troops, including Russian forces; during that time the square was named Stalinplatz after the Soviet dictator.

In the distance beyond the prince, at the far end of the long square, look for a fountain with a tall monument and a big colonnade just behind it. This **Russian monument** was built in 1945 as a forced thank-you to the Soviets for liberating Austria from the Nazis. Formerly a sore point, now the monument is just ignored.

❷ Schwarzenbergplatz

Three blocks ahead, on the right, is the huge **Stadtpark** or City Park. This inviting green space honors many great Viennese musicians and composers with statues. At the beginning of the park, the gold-and-cream concert hall behind the trees is the **Kursalon,** opened in 1867 by the Strauss brothers, who directed many waltzes here. Touristy Strauss concerts are held in this building (for details, see the Activities chapter). If the weather's nice, you could hop off at the next stop for a stroll in Vienna's finest park.

A glimpse of the Russian monument

Stadtpark, one of Vienna's green spaces

❸ **Weihburggasse**

On the right, immediately after this stop, in the park but barely visible from the tram is a gilded tribute to "Waltz King" **Johann Strauss** (squint through the park gate a few yards beyond the stop to find a statue under a white arch). He holds a violin as he did when he conducted his orchestra, whipping his fans into a three-quarter-time frenzy.

❹ **Stubentor**

On the left (immediately across from the stop), centered in a public square, is a bronze statue (now green but likely covered with graffiti) of **Dr. Karl Lueger.** The mayor from 1897 to 1910, he shaped Vienna into a modern city. Once hugely popular and influential, his anti-Semitism has caught up with him and this statue may be gone, as he's being canceled by Vienna (see "The Birth of Modern Vienna" sidebar, later).

Immediately after the Lueger statue and across the street, look right at the big, red-brick building. This is the **MAK** (Museum of Applied Arts), showing furniture and design through the ages.

A block after the museum (still on the right), the long, white building used to be the **Austrian Ministry of War,** back when that

Johann Strauss gets a statue in Stadtpark, near the Kursalon where his waltzes still play.

The Museum of Applied Arts (MAK)   The Postal Savings Bank, by Otto Wagner

was a major operation. Above its oval windows, you can see busts of soldiers, wearing Stratego-style military helmets. Each shows the uniform of a different regiment and the folkloric tradition of its country within the Habsburg realm.

To the left, directly across the street from the start of the Ministry of War, is the **Postal Savings Bank** (set back on a little square, in a little gap between the buildings). Designed by Otto Wagner, it's one of the rare Secessionist buildings facing the Ring. (For more on the Secession, see the sidebar on page 140.)

❺ Julius-Raab-Platz

Immediately after this stop, the tram makes a sharp left turn. To the right is the white dome of the **Urania,** Franz Josef's 1910 observatory. And in the distance, you may see the famous giant Ferris wheel. Erected in 1897 as the centerpiece of the beloved Prater amusement park, it is 212 feet high and was the world's tallest until 1985. OK! Get ready to hop off for your transfer at the next stop.

❻ Schwedenplatz (Get off Tram #2 and View the Canal)

Hop off tram #2 and find the platform for tram #1. (You get off at track A and hop on at track B—the next track over, a few feet closer to the town center and farther from the canal.) Notice tram #1 arrival times on the monitor. They'll come every five or ten minutes, so feel free to take a break here before boarding tram #1 to finish your Ringstrasse loop.

For a good viewpoint, cross the street and climb up the wooden stairs of **Motto am Fluss,** the recommended restaurant immediately opposite the tram stop and overlooking the canal.

The domed Urania, part of the parade of architectural styles on the Ring from circa 1900

The waterway is the **Danube Canal** (a.k.a. the "Baby Danube"), one of the many small arms of the river that once made up the Danube at this location. The rest have been gathered in a mightier modern-day Danube, farther away. The river was engineered for stability and trade in 1873.

This area was once the center and harbor of the original Roman town, Vindobona. Located on the banks of the Danube, Vindobona marked the end of the civilized world. To the north lay the barbarian (non-Latin-speaking) Germanic lands.

To the far left are the Vienna Woods and the foothills of the Alps. From this point the Alps arc across Europe all the way to the French Riviera where they plunge into the Mediterranean. The embankment has become a lazy park-like people-zone with restaurant boats, swimming pools, sundecks, bars with lounge chairs for sunning, and bike paths stretching in both directions.

The modern boat station (located where the original Roman harbor was) is the terminal for the fast boat to Bratislava, the capital city of Slovakia, about an hour away downstream.

If some of the buildings across the canal seem a bit drab, that's

While you wait between trams for Part II of our tour, enjoy a placid branch of the mighty Danube.

because in April 1945, the last month of World War II, this prime real estate was bombed. Postwar buildings were constructed on the cheap and are now being replaced by sleek, futuristic buildings. (The tall black skyscraper houses the Sofitel with an elegant view restaurant on top. And beyond that are a few delightful recommended restaurants.)

By the way, this square is called Schwedenplatz ("Sweden Square") because after World War I, Vienna was overwhelmed with hungry orphans. The Swedes took several thousand in, raised them, and finally sent them home healthy and well-fed.

❼ Schwedenplatz (Hop on Tram #1)

Get ready—here comes tram #1, heading in the same direction you've been going. (If you're waiting a few minutes for it to arrive, read ahead to the next section.) Hopping a tram here, I like to grab a seat on the left. After three blocks, on the left, you'll see the ivy-covered walls and round Romanesque arches of **St. Ruprecht's** (Ruprechtskirche), the oldest church in Vienna. It was built in the 11th century on a bit of Roman ruins. Beyond that is a nightclub quarter nicknamed "The Bermuda Triangle."

❽ Salztorbrücke

As there's not much to see until after the next stop (you'll pass the

Salztorbrücke stop and continue on to Schottenring), spend a couple of minutes reading ahead.

It's interesting to remember that the Ringstrasse replaced the mighty walls that once protected Vienna from external enemies.

Imagine the great imperial capital contained within its three-mile-long wall, most of which dated from the 16th to 18th century. As was typical of city walls, it was lined with cannons (2,200, in Vienna's case) and surrounded by a "shooting field" or "cannonball zone." This swath of land, as wide as a cannonball could fly (about 400 yards), was clear-cut so no one could approach without being seen...and targeted.

After the popular unrest and uprisings of 1848, the emperor realized the true threat against him was from inside. He rid the city of its walls in about 1860, built this boulevard and transportation infrastructure (useful for moving citizens in good times and soldiers in bad), and, as you'll see in a moment, he moved his army closer at hand. Napoleon III's remodel of Paris demonstrated that wide boulevards make it impossible for revolutionaries to erect barricades to block the movement of people and supplies. That encouraged Franz Josef to implement a similarly broad street plan for his Ring. A straight stretch of boulevard may seem just stately, but for an embattled emperor, it's an easy-to-defend corridor.

Vienna's wall survived longer than those in most European capital cities because its Old Regime rulers did. When the emperor had the walls taken down, the shooting field was wide open and ripe for development. That's why the wonderful architecture that lines the outer edge of the Ringstrasse is all from the same era (post-1860).

❾ Schottenring

After this stop, the tram leaves the canal and turns left. Through a gap in the buildings, you'll get a glimpse of a huge, red-brick castle—actually high-profile **barracks** for 6,000 troops built here at the command of a nervous Emperor Franz Josef (who found himself on the throne as an 18-year-old in 1848, the same year people's revolts against autocracy were sweeping across Europe). Today this is the headquarters of the National Defense.

❿ Börse

At the stop look left to see the orange-and-white, Neo-Renaissance temple of money—the **Börse** was Vienna's stock exchange. The next block

The Birth of Modern Vienna

As Vienna's population grew in the 1800s from 500,000 to more than 2 million, the city needed to expand. The old medieval wall was torn down to create the Ringstrasse. The street was lined with leafy parks and Vienna's most important buildings—City Hall, Parliament, stock exchange, the ritziest cafés, the theater, art museum, and opera house. Back then, gas lamps lit the night, and horse-drawn trams clip-clopped under the trees. Buildings were state of the art, but decorated in styles that echoed the past (often called "Historicism"). Some were Neoclassical—with Greek columns and Roman arches; others were Neo-Gothic, with the look of a medieval church, and so on.

Besides the Ring, the rest of Vienna was transformed in the late 1800s. The old water system of Roman-style aqueducts was replaced with modern plumbing. Thomas Edison was hired to install electric lights at Schönbrunn Palace. The Danube was tamed with flood controls. Engineers even began an artificial island that eventually became Danube Island.

Vienna's incredible transformation was overseen by three people: Emperor Franz Josef (who ruled for 68 years during Vienna's golden age), Mayor Karl Lueger, and chief architect Otto Wagner. In a few short decades, they turned the Ringstrasse—and Vienna—into the wonder of Europe. But Lueger himself has fallen into disrepute because of his racist politics. The part of the Ring named after him was rechristened the Universitätsring in 2012, and many would like to see his statue near the Stubentor stop removed as well.

is lined with banks and insurance companies—the financial district of Austria, though many of these flashy financial institutions have sold and moved out to more modern and less central locations (for example, the former Rothschild bank building now houses a big Spar supermarket).

After the corner, look right for the towering, frilly, Neo-Gothic church across the small park. This is a **"votive church,"** a type of church built to fulfill a vow in thanks for God's help—in this case, expressing gratitude for the failure of an 1853 assassination attempt on Emperor Franz Josef.

Look left and right to see the fine lines of buildings (two blocks on the left, three on the right) built in the free-fire zone of the wall after

1870. This string of grand, late-19th-century buildings stretches three miles along the real estate freed up with the demolition of the wall. What a gift to developers!

⓫ Schottentor

Leaving this stop, on the right is the main building of the **University of Vienna** (Universität Wien). Established in 1365, the university has no real campus, as its buildings are scattered around town. It's considered the oldest continuously operating university in the German-speaking world and has nearly 100,000 students.

Immediately opposite the university, on the left, a chunk of the old **city wall** is visible (behind a monument topped with a gilded angel). The seated female statue under the trees is a monument to the Trümmerfrauen, "rubble women" who helped clear and rebuild Vienna brick by brick after World War II. Beethoven lived and composed in the building just above the piece of wall. Imagine, he wrote "Für Elise" right here.

The City Hall, with its Neo-Gothic spires, hosts a food circus and entertainment in summer.

⓬ Rathausplatz/Burgtheater

At the stop, on the right, you'll see how the Neo-Gothic **City Hall** (Rathaus) flies both the local flag and the flag of Europe. The square in front (Rathausplatz) is a festive site in summer, with a thriving food circus and a huge screen showing outdoor movies, operas, and concerts (described in the Activities chapter).

Opposite that on the left is the **Burgtheater,** Austria's national theater. Locals brag it's the "leading theater in the German-speaking world."

⓭ Parliament

On the right, you can't miss the temple of democracy housing the **Austrian Parliament.** The lady with the golden helmet is Athena, goddess of wisdom. Across the street from the Parliament (on the left) is the imperial park called the **Volksgarten,** with a fine public rose garden.

⓮ Ring/Volkstheater

The vast building (on the right) is the **Natural History Museum** (Naturhistorisches Museum), which faces its twin, the **Kunsthistorisches Museum,** containing the city's greatest collection of paintings. The **MuseumsQuartier** behind them completes the ensemble with a collection of modern art museums. A hefty statue of Empress **Maria Theresa** squats between the museums, facing the grand gate to the Hofburg Palace.

Opposite Maria Theresa (look left), the arched gate (the only surviving castle gate of the old town wall, its current iteration built to celebrate the 1824 victory over Napoleon) leads to the **Hofburg,** the

The Burgtheater, still a working theater

Parliament, with its statue of Athena

emperor's palace. Of the five arches, the center one was used only by the emperor.

Your tour is nearly finished. Consider hopping off here to visit the Hofburg or the Kunsthistorisches Museum.

⓯ Burgring

Until 1918, the appealing **Burggarten** (on the left) was the private garden of the emperor. Today locals enjoy relaxing here, and it's also home to a famous statue of **Mozart** (hard to see from the tram—he's hiding behind the leaves).

On the right is the **Burg Kino** theater, which plays the movie *The Third Man* several times a week in English (see page 160).

A hundred yards farther (on the left, just after the park), the German philosopher **Goethe** sits in a big, thought-provoking chair. Goethe seems to be playing trivia with German poet **Schiller** across the street (in the little park set back from the street, on your right). Behind the statue of Schiller is the **Academy of Fine Arts** (described in the Sights chapter).

The next stop is our last. We're back where we started—the opera—and it's time to get out.

⓰ Oper/Karlsplatz—Whew!

Jump off the tram and see the rest of the city. To join me on a walking tour of Vienna's center, which starts here at the opera, 📖 see the Vienna City Walk chapter. Or spend another 30 minutes making this loop again to see all the things you missed.

The Kunsthistorisches—fine Historicism

It's been a blur, but a good overview.

Hofburg Imperial Apartments Tour

In this tour of the Hofburg Imperial Apartments, you'll see the lavish rooms that were home to the hardworking Emperor Franz Josef I and his eccentric empress, "Sisi." From here, the Habsburgs ruled their vast empire.

Franz Josef was the last of the great Habsburg monarchs, and these apartments straddle the transition from old to new. You'll see chandeliered luxury alongside office furniture and electric lights.

Franz Josef and Sisi were also a study in contrasts. Where Franz was earnest, practical, and spartan, Sisi was poetic, high-strung, and luxury-loving. Together, they lived in the cocoon of the Imperial Apartments, seemingly oblivious to how the world was changing around them.

The Hofburg, home of emperors for 600 years, and now the office of the Austrian president

ORIENTATION

Cost: €16, includes well-done audioguide; also covered by Sisi Ticket, which includes the Schönbrunn Palace Grand Tour and the Vienna Furniture Museum (Sisi Ticket described on page 126). To avoid lines, buy your Sisi Ticket at the Vienna Furniture Museum or online (see below).

Hours: Daily 9:00-17:30, July-Aug until 18:00, last entry one hour before closing.

Information: +43 1 533 7570, www.sisimuseum-hofburg.at.

When to Go: Visit either right at opening time or after 14:00.

Getting There: Enter from under the rotunda just off Michaelerplatz, through the Michaelertor gate.

Tours: Guided English tours (€4) run daily at 14:00. The included audioguide brings the exhibit to life.

Length of This Tour: If you listen to the entire audioguide, allow 40 minutes for the porcelain and silver collection, 30 minutes for the Sisi Museum, and 40 minutes for the apartments.

THE TOUR BEGINS

The Imperial Apartments are part of the large Hofburg Palace complex. Your ticket grants you admission to three separate exhibits, which you'll visit on a one-way route. The first floor holds a collection of precious porcelain and silver knickknacks (*Silberkammer*). You then go upstairs to the Sisi Museum, which has displays about her life. This leads into the 20 or so rooms of the Imperial Apartments (*Kaiserappartements*), starting in Franz Josef's rooms, then heading into the dozen rooms where his wife Sisi lived.

Imperial Porcelain and Silver Collection

▶ *Your visit (and the excellent audioguide) starts on the ground floor.*

Tableware Collection

The audioguide actually manages to make the Habsburg court's vast tableware collection interesting. The cabinets are full (with the contents intact—this area was never bombed), and the displays were functional so that servants could select the proper items, as the royals

Hofburg Imperial Apartments Tour

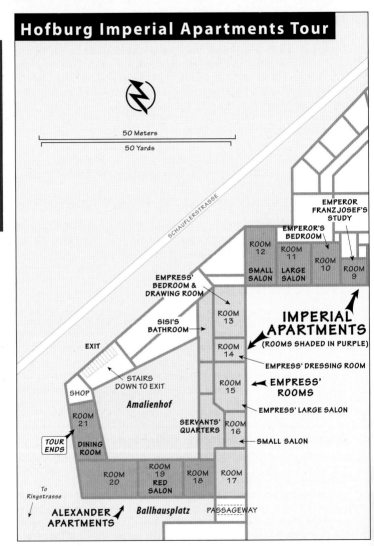

50 Meters

50 Yards

SCHAUFLERSTRASSE

EMPEROR
FRANZ JOSEF'S
STUDY

EMPEROR'S
BEDROOM

ROOM 12

ROOM 11

ROOM 10

ROOM 9

SMALL SALON

LARGE SALON

EMPRESS'
BEDROOM &
DRAWING ROOM

SISI'S
BATHROOM

ROOM 13

IMPERIAL
APARTMENTS

(ROOMS SHADED IN PURPLE)

EXIT

ROOM 14

EMPRESS' DRESSING ROOM

STAIRS
DOWN TO EXIT

ROOM 15

EMPRESS'
ROOMS

SHOP

Amalienhof

EMPRESS' LARGE SALON

ROOM 21

SERVANTS'
QUARTERS

ROOM 16

SMALL SALON

TOUR
ENDS

DINING
ROOM

To
Ringstrasse

ROOM 20

ROOM 19
RED SALON

ROOM 18

ROOM 17

ALEXANDER
APARTMENTS

Ballhausplatz

PASSAGEWAY

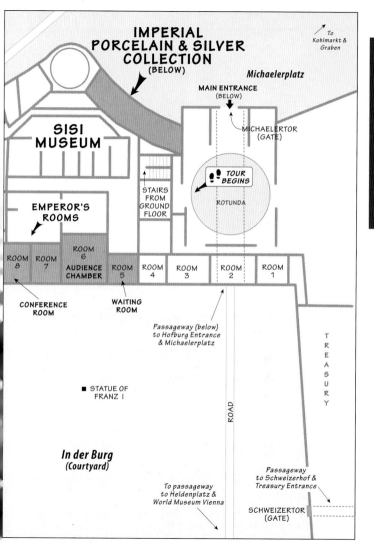

IMPERIAL PORCELAIN & SILVER COLLECTION (BELOW)

Michaelerplatz

To Kohlmarkt & Graben

MAIN ENTRANCE (BELOW)

MICHAELERTOR (GATE)

SISI MUSEUM

STAIRS FROM GROUND FLOOR

TOUR BEGINS

ROTUNDA

EMPEROR'S ROOMS

| ROOM 8 | ROOM 7 | ROOM 6 AUDIENCE CHAMBER | ROOM 5 | ROOM 4 | ROOM 3 | ROOM 2 | ROOM 1 |

CONFERENCE ROOM

WAITING ROOM

Passageway (below) to Hofburg Entrance & Michaelerplatz

TREASURY

■ STATUE OF FRANZ I

ROAD

In der Burg (Courtyard)

To passageway to Heldenplatz & World Museum Vienna

Passageway to Schweizerhof & Treasury Entrance

SCHWEIZERTOR (GATE)

The visit begins with imperial porcelain.

The audioguide brings exhibits to life.

would entertain up to 800 guests at a time. Gawk at the opulence and take in some colorful Habsburg trivia. (Who'da thunk that the court had an official way to fold a napkin—and that the technique remains a closely guarded secret?) Still, I wouldn't bog down here, as there's much more to see upstairs.

▶ *Once you're through all those rooms of dishes, climb the same stairs used by the emperors and empresses who lived here. At the top is a timeline of Sisi's life. Swipe your ticket to pass through the turnstile, consider the rare WC, and enter the room with the...*

Model of the Hofburg

Circle to the far side to find where you're standing right now, near the Hofburg's largest dome. That dome tops the entrance to the Hofburg from Michaelerplatz.

The Hofburg was the epicenter of one of Europe's great political powers—600 years of Habsburgs lived here. The Hofburg started as a 13th-century medieval castle (near where you are right now) and expanded over the centuries to today's 240,000-square-meter (60-acre) complex, now owned by the state.

To the left of the dome (as you face the facade) is the steeple of the Augustinian Church. It was there, in 1854, that Franz Josef married 16-year-old Elisabeth of Bavaria, and their story began.

▶ *Now enter a darkened room at the beginning of the...*

Sisi Museum

Empress Elisabeth (1837-1898)—a.k.a. "Sisi" (SEE-see)—was Franz Josef's mysterious, beautiful, and narcissistic wife. This museum

Sisi (1837-1898)

Empress Elisabeth was the 19th-century equivalent of Princess Diana. Known as "Sisi" since childhood, she became an instant celebrity when she married Franz Josef at 16. Franz Josef was supposed to have married Sisi's sister, but he married Sisi instead—for love.

Sisi's main goals in life seem to have been preserving her reputation as a beautiful empress, maintaining her Barbie-doll figure, and tending to her fairy-tale, ankle-length hair. But, despite severe dieting and fanatical exercise, age took its toll. After turning 30, she refused to allow photographs or portraits, and was generally seen in public with a delicate fan covering her face (and bad teeth).

Politically, Sisi's personal cause was promoting Hungary's bid for autonomy within the empire. Her personal tragedy was the death of her son Rudolf, the crown prince, in an apparent suicide (an incident often dramatized as the "Mayerling Affair"). Disliking Vienna and the confines of the court, Sisi traveled more and more frequently. As the years passed, the restless Sisi and her hardworking husband became estranged. In 1898, while visiting Geneva, Switzerland, she was murdered by an Italian anarchist.

traces her fabulous but tragic life with the help of her flowery poetry, which is posted for reading as you stroll through these ornate halls.

Sisi's Death

The exhibit starts with Sisi's sad end, showing her **death mask,** photos of her **funeral procession** (by the Hercules statues facing Michaelerplatz), and an **engraving** of a grieving Franz Josef. It was at her death that the obscure, private empress' legend began to grow.

▶ *Continue into the corridor.*

The Sisi Myth

Sisi was not a major public figure in her lifetime, as **newspaper clippings** of the day make clear. She was often absent from public

The Sisi Museum introduces you to this complicated character; then you tour her living quarters.

functions, and the censored press was gagged from reporting on her eccentricities. After her death, however, her image quickly became a commodity and began appearing on everyday items such as **candy tins** and **beer steins.**

The plaster-cast life-sized **statue** captures the one element of her persona everyone knew: her beauty. Sisi was nearly 5'8" (a head taller than her husband), had a 20-inch waist (she wore very tight corsets), and weighed only about 100 pounds. (Her waistline eventually grew… to 21 inches. That was at age 50, after giving birth to four children.) This statue, a copy of one of 30 statues that were erected in her honor in European cities, shows her holding one of her trademark fans. It doesn't show off her magnificent hair, however, which reached down as far as her ankles in her youth.

Sisi-mania really got going in the 1950s with a series of **movies** based on her life (starring Romy Schneider), depicting the empress as beautiful and innocent, and either crying or singing at any given point in the films.

▶ *Round the corner into the next room.*

Sisi's Childhood

Sisi grew up in Bavaria, far from sophisticated city life. (See her **baby shoes** in a box and the picture of her **childhood palace**.) Franz Josef—who'd been engaged to her older sister—spied seemingly happy-go-lucky Sisi when she was 15 and fell in love. They married. At the wedding reception, Sisi burst into tears, the first sign that something was not right.

The Ballroom: Sisi at Court

In the glass display cases are replicas of her **gowns.** Big **portraits** of Sisi (considered the most realistic in existence) and Franz Josef show them dressed to the nines. **Jewels** (also replicas) reproduce some of the finery she wore as empress—but to her, they were her "chains." She hated official court duties, the constraints of public life, and being the center of attention. Sisi's mother-in-law dominated her child-rearing, her first-born died as an infant, and she complained that she couldn't sleep or eat. However, she did participate in one political cause—championing the rights of Habsburg-controlled Hungary (see her **bust** and **portrait as Queen of Hungary**).

▶ *Head into the next, darkened room.*

Sisi's Beauty

Sisi longed for the carefree days of her youth. She began to withdraw from public life, passing time riding horses (see **horse** statuettes and pictures) and tending obsessively to maintaining her physical beauty. In the glass case on the right wall, you'll see some of her **menus,** and a **bill from Demel.** Her **recipes** for beauty preparations included creams and lotions as well as wearing a raw-meat face mask while she slept. Sisi weighed herself obsessively on her gold-trimmed **scale** and tried all types of diets, including bouillon made with a **duck press.** (She never gave up pastries and ice cream, however.) After she turned 30, Sisi refused to appear in any portraits or photographs, preferring that only her more youthful depictions be preserved. Appreciate the **white gloves,** the **ivory fan,** and the **white nightgown** (displayed nearby)...because her life was about to turn even more dark.

▶ *Then enter the darkest room.*

Death of Sisi's Son

A mannequin wears a replica of Sisi's **black dress,** and nearby you'll see **black jewels** and accessories. In 1889, Sisi and Franz Josef's son, Prince Rudolf—whose life had veered into sex, drugs, and liberal politics—apparently killed his lover and himself. Sisi was shattered and retreated further from public life.

▶ *Stroll through several more rooms.*

Escape

Sisi consoled herself with **poetry** (the museum has quotes on the walls) that expresses a longing to escape into an ideal world. As you continue through the exhibit, you'll see she also consoled herself with travel. There's a reconstruction of her **rail car.** A **map** shows her visits to Britain, Eastern Europe, and her favorite spot, Greece.

Final Room: Assassination

Sisi met her fate while traveling. While walking along a street in Geneva, Sisi was stalked and attacked by an Italian anarchist who despised royal oppressors and wanted notoriety for his cause. (He'd planned on assassinating a less-famous French prince that day—whom he'd been unable to track down—but quickly changed plans when word got out that Sisi was in town.) The murder weapon was a small, crude, knife-like file. It made only a small wound, but it proved fatal.

▶ *After the Sisi Museum, a one-way route takes you through a series of royal rooms. The first room—as if to make clear that there was more to the Habsburgs than Sisi—shows a family tree tracing the Habsburgs from 1273 (Rudolf I at upper left) to their messy WWI demise (Karl I, lower right). From here, enter the private apartments of the royal family. Much of the following commentary complements the information you'll hear in the audioguide.*

Imperial Apartments

These were the private apartments and public meeting rooms for the emperor and empress. Franz Josef I lived here from 1857 until his death in 1916. (He had hoped to move to new digs in the Neue Burg, but that was not finished until after his death.)

Franz Josef was the last legendary Habsburg. In these rooms, he presided over defeats and liberal inroads as the world was changing and the monarchy becoming obsolete. Here he met with advisors and welcomed foreign dignitaries; hosted lavish, white-gloved balls and stuffy formal dinners; and raised his children. He slept (alone) on his

Each of the rooms features a different variation on chandeliered, stuccoed opulence.

austere bed while his beloved wife Sisi retreated to her own rooms. He suffered through the execution of his brother, the suicide of his son and heir, the murder of his wife, and the assassination of his nephew, Archduke Ferdinand, which sparked World War I and spelled the end of the Habsburg Monarchy.

The Emperor's Rooms
Waiting Room for the Audience Chamber

Every citizen had the right to meet privately with the emperor, and people traveled far to do so. While they waited nervously, they had these **three huge paintings** to stare at—propaganda art showing crowds of commoners enthusiastic about their Habsburg rulers.

The painting on the right shows an 1809 scene of Emperor Franz II (Franz Josef's grandfather) returning to Vienna, celebrating the news that Napoleon had begun his retreat.

In the central painting, Franz II makes his first public appearance to adoring crowds after recovering from a life-threatening illness (1826).

In the painting on the left, Franz II returns to Vienna to celebrate the defeat of Napoleon. The 1815 Congress of Vienna that followed

Emperor Franz Josef (1830-1916)

Franz Josef I—who ruled for 68 years (1848-1916)—was the embodiment of the Habsburg Empire as it finished its six-century-long ride. Born in 1830, Franz Josef had a stern upbringing that instilled in him a powerful sense of duty and a love of all things military.

As the revolutions of 1848 rattled royal families throughout Europe, the Habsburgs forced Ferdinand to abdicate and put 18-year-old Franz Josef on the throne. One of his first acts put down the 1848 revolt in Hungary with bloody harshness.

Rather than acknowledge the changing world around him, Franz Josef became very conservative. But worse, he wrongly believed he was a talented military tactician, leading Austria into catastrophic battles against Italy.

Wearing his uniform to the end, Franz Josef never saw what a dinosaur his monarchy was becoming. He had no interest in democracy and pointedly never set foot in Austria's parliament building. Like his contemporary, Queen Victoria, he was a microcosm of his empire—old-fashioned and sacrosanct. Mired in his passion for low-grade paperwork (which earned him the nickname "Joe Bureaucrat"), he missed the big picture. In 1914, he helped start a Great War that ultimately ended the age of monarchs.

was the greatest assembly of diplomats in European history. Its goal: to establish peace by shoring up Europe's monarchies against the rise of democracy and nationalism. It worked for about a century, until a colossal war—World War I—wiped out the Habsburgs and other European royal families.

This room's **chandelier**—considered the best in the palace—is Baroque, made of Bohemian crystal. It lit things until 1891, when the palace installed electric lights.

Audience Chamber

This is the room where Franz Josef received commoners from around the empire. Imagine you've traveled for days to have your say before the emperor. You're wearing your new fancy suit—Franz Josef required that men coming before him wear a tailcoat, women a black gown with a train. You've rehearsed what you want to say. You hope your hair looks good.

Suddenly, you're face-to-face with the emp himself. (The **portrait** on the easel shows Franz Josef in 1915, when he was more than 80 years old.) He'd stand at the lectern (far left) as the visiting commoners had their say (but for no more than two-and-a-half minutes). You'd hear a brief response from him (quite likely the same he'd given all day), and then you'd back out of the room while bowing (also required). On the **lectern** is a partial list of 56 appointments he had on January 3, 1910 (three columns: family name, meeting topic, and *Anmerkung*—the emperor's "action log").

Conference Room

The emperor and his cabinet sat at this long Empire-style table to discuss policy. An ongoing topic was what to do with unruly Hungary. After 1867, Franz Josef granted Hungary a measure of independence (thus creating the "Austro-Hungarian Empire"). Hungarian diplomats attended meetings here, watched over by **paintings** on the wall showing Austria's army suppressing the popular Hungarian uprising... subtle.

Emperor Franz Josef's Study

This room evokes how seriously the emperor took his responsibilities as the top official of a vast empire. Famously energetic, Franz Josef lived a spartan life dedicated to duty. The **desk** was originally positioned in such a way that he could look up from his work and see the **portrait** of Sisi reflected in the mirror. Notice the **trompe l'oeil paintings** above each door, giving the believable illusion of marble relief. Notice also all the **family photos**—the perfect gift for the dad/uncle/hubby who has it all.

The walls between the rooms are wide enough to hide servants' corridors (the hidden door to his valet's room is in the back-left corner). The emperor lived with a personal staff of 14: "three valets, four lackeys, two doormen, two manservants, and three chambermaids."

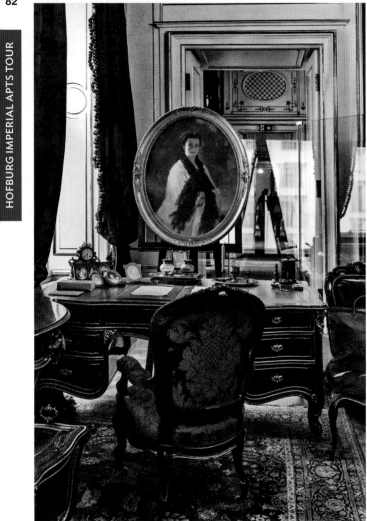

Franz Josef adored Sisi, and kept reminders of her everywhere—like on his office desk.

Emperor's Bedroom

Franz Josef famously slept on this no-frills **iron bed** and used the **portable washstand** until 1880 (when the palace got running water). He typically rose before dawn and started his day in prayer, kneeling at the **prayer stool** against the far wall. After all, he was a "Divine Right" ruler. While he had a typical emperor's share of mistresses, his dresser was always well-stocked with **photos** of Sisi, even after their estrangement. An **etching** shows the empress (dressed in black after the 1889 suicide of her son)—a fine rider and avid hunter—sitting side-saddle while jumping a hedge.

Large Salon

This red-walled room was for royal family gatherings and went un-used after Sisi's death. The big, ornate **stove** in the corner was fed from behind (this remained a standard form of heating through the 19th century).

Small Salon

This room is dedicated to the memory of Franz Josef's brother (see the **portrait with the weird beard**), Emperor Maximilian I of Mexico, who was overthrown and executed in 1867. It was also a smoking room. This was a necessity in the early 19th century, when smoking was newly fashionable for men, and was never done in the presence of women.

After the birth of their last child in 1868, Franz Josef and Sisi be-gan to drift further apart. Left of the door is a small **button** the em-peror had to buzz before entering his estranged wife's quarters. You, however, can go right in.

▶ *Enter Sisi's wing.*

Empress' Rooms

Empress' Bedroom and Drawing Room

This was Sisi's room, refurbished in the Neo-Rococo style in 1854. The room always had lots of fresh flowers. Sisi not only slept here, but also lived here—the bed was rolled in and out daily—until her death in 1898. The **desk** is where she sat and wrote her letters and sad poems.

Empress' Dressing/Exercise Room

Servants worked three hours a day on Sisi's famous hair, while she

Carpets, divans, and ceramic furnaces gave state-of-the-art comfort.

passed the time reading and learning Hungarian. She'd exercise on the **wooden structure** and on the **rings** suspended from the doorway to the left. Afterward, she'd get a massage on the red-covered **bed.** You can psychoanalyze Sisi from the **portraits and photos** she chose to hang on her walls. They're mostly her favorite dogs, her Bavarian family, and several portraits of the romantic and anti-monarchist poet Heinrich Heine. Her infatuation with the liberal Heine, whose family was Jewish, caused a stir in royal circles.

Empress' Lavatory and Bathroom

Detour into the behind-the-scenes palace. In the narrow passageway, you'll walk by Sisi's hand-painted porcelain, dolphin-head **WC** (on the right). The big tank left of the tub warmed her towels. In the main bathroom, you'll see her huge copper tub (with the original wall coverings behind it), where servants washed her hair. Sisi was the first Habsburg to have running water in her bathroom (notice the hot and cold faucets).

Servants' Quarters (Bergl Rooms)

Next, enter the servants' quarters, with hand-painted **tropical scenes.** Take time to enjoy the playful details. As you leave these rooms and reenter the imperial world, look back (through an open door) to the room on the left.

Empress' Large Salon

The room is painted with **Mediterranean escapes,** the 19th-century equivalent of travel posters. Franz Josef and Sisi would—on their good days—share breakfast in this room.

Small Salon

The portrait is of **Crown Prince Rudolf,** Franz Josef's and Sisi's only son. On the morning of January 30, 1889, the 30-year-old Rudolf and a beautiful baroness were found shot dead in his hunting lodge in Mayerling. An investigation never came up with a complete explanation, but Rudolf had obviously been cheating on his wife, and the affair ended in an apparent murder-suicide. The scandal shocked the empire and tainted the Habsburgs; Sisi retreated further into her fantasy world, and Franz Josef carried on stoically with a broken heart. The mysterious "Mayerling Affair" has been dramatized in numerous movies, plays, an opera, and even a ballet.

▶ *Leaving Sisi's wing, turn the corner into the white-and-gold rooms occupied by the czar of Russia during the 1814-1815 Congress of Vienna. Sisi and Franz Josef used the rooms for formal occasions and public functions.*

Alexander Apartments

In these apartments—named for the tapestries of Alexander the Great that once adorned the walls—Empress Sisi would host dinners and receptions for her guests.

Red Salon

The Gobelin wall hangings (one of the four is an original) were a 1776 gift from Marie-Antoinette and Louis XVI in Paris to their Viennese counterparts.

Dining Room

It's dinnertime, and Franz Josef has called his extended family together. The settings are modest...just silver. Gold was saved for formal state dinners. Next to each name card was a menu listing the chef responsible for each dish. (Talk about pressure.) While the Hofburg had

The dining room hosted heads of state as well as the emperor's large extended family.

tableware for 4,000, feeding 3,000 was a typical day. The cellar was stocked with 60,000 bottles of wine. The kitchen was huge—50 birds could be roasted at once on the hand-turned spits.

The emperor sat in the center of the long table. "Ladies and gentlemen" alternated in the seating. The green glasses were specifically for Rhenish wine (dry whites from the Rhine valley). Franz Josef enforced strict protocol at mealtime: No one could speak without being spoken to by the emperor, and no one could eat after he was done. While the rest of Europe was growing democracy and expanding personal freedoms, the Habsburgs preserved their ossified worldview to the bitter end.

In 1918, World War I ended, Austria was created as a modern nation-state, the Habsburgs were tossed out...and Hofburg Palace was destined to become the museum you've just toured.

▶ *Drop off your audioguide, zip through the shop, go down the stairs, and you're back on the street. Two quick lefts take you back to the palace square (In der Burg), where the Treasury awaits just past the black, red, and gold gate on the far side (see the next chapter).*

Hofburg
Treasury Tour

The Hofburg Palace's Imperial Treasury contains the best jewels on the Continent. Slip through the vault doors and reflect on the glitter of 21 rooms filled with secular and religious ornaments: scepters, swords, crowns, orbs, weighty robes, double-headed eagles, gowns, gem-studded bangles, and a unicorn horn.

There are plenty of beautiful objects here—I've highlighted those that have the most history behind them. But you could spend hours in here marveling at the riches of the bygone empire.

Use this chapter to get the lay of the land, but renting the excellent audioguide gives you a deeper explanation of these historic jewels.

ORIENTATION

Cost: €14, €24 combo-ticket with Kunsthistorisches Museum.

Hours: Wed-Mon 9:00-17:30, closed Tue.

Information: +43 1 525 240, www.kaiserliche-schatzkammer.at.

Getting There: The Treasury is tucked away in the Hofburg Palace complex. From the Hofburg's central courtyard (In der Burg), pass through the black, red, and gold gate (Schweizertor), following *Schatzkammer* signs, which lead into the Schweizerhof courtyard; the Treasury entrance is in the far-right corner.

Tours: The €5 audioguide (€7/2 people) describes 100 stops—well worth it to get the most out of this dazzling collection.

Starring: The Imperial Crown and other accessories of the Holy Roman Emperors, plus many other crowns, jewels, robes, and priceless knickknacks.

THE TOUR BEGINS

The Habsburgs saw themselves as the successors to the ancient Roman emperors, and they wanted crowns and royal regalia to match the pomp of the ancients. They used these precious objects for coronation ceremonies, official ribbon-cutting events, and their own personal pleasure. You'll see the prestigious crowns and accoutrements of the rulers of the Holy Roman Empire (a medieval alliance of Germanic kingdoms so named because it wanted to be considered the continuation of the Roman Empire). Other crowns belonged to Austrian dukes and kings, and some robes and paraphernalia were used by Austria's religious elite. And many costly things were created simply for the enjoyment of the wealthy Habsburgs.

▶ *Skip through Room 1 to where we'll begin, in Room 2.*

From the First Habsburg to Napoleon

Room 2

The personal ❶ **crown of Rudolf II** (1602) occupies the center of the room along with its accompanying scepter and orb; a bust of Rudolf II (1552-1612) sits nearby. The crown's design symbolically merges a bishop's miter ("Holy"), the arch across the top of a Roman emperor's

Hofburg Treasury Tour

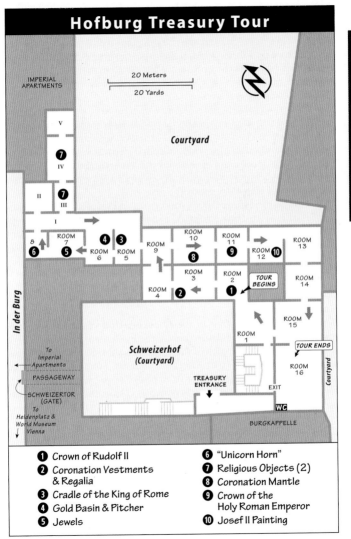

1 Crown of Rudolf II
2 Coronation Vestments & Regalia
3 Cradle of the King of Rome
4 Gold Basin & Pitcher
5 Jewels
6 "Unicorn Horn"
7 Religious Objects (2)
8 Coronation Mantle
9 Crown of the Holy Roman Emperor
10 Josef II Painting

helmet ("Roman"), and the typical medieval king's crown ("Emperor"). Accompanying the crown are the matching **scepter** (made from the ivory tusk of a narwhal) and **orb** (holding four diamonds to symbolize the four corners of the world, which the emperor ruled). Orbs have been royal symbols of the world since ancient Roman times. They seem to indicate that, even in pre-Columbus days, Europe's intelligentsia assumed the world was round.

This crown was Rudolf's personal one. He wore a different crown (which we'll see later) in his official role as Holy Roman Emperor. In many dynasties, a personal crown like this was dismantled by the next ruler to custom-make his own. But Rudolf's crown was so well-crafted that it was passed down through the generations, even inspiring crown-shaped church steeples as far away as Amsterdam (when that city was under Habsburg control).

Two centuries later (1806), this crown and scepter became the official regalia of Austria's rulers, as seen in the large **portrait of Franz I** (the open-legged guy behind you). Napoleon Bonaparte had just conquered Austria and dissolved the Holy Roman Empire. Franz (r. 1792-1835) was allowed to remain in power, but he had to downgrade his title from "Franz II, Holy Roman Emperor" to "Franz I, Emperor of Austria."

Rooms 3 and 4

These rooms contain some of the ❷ **coronation vestments and regalia** needed for the new Austrian (not Holy Roman) Emperor. There was a different one for each of the emperor's subsidiary titles—for example, King of Hungary or King of Lombardy. So many crowns and kingdoms in the Habsburgs' vast empire! Those with the white ermine collars are modeled after Napoleon's coronation robes. Sketches on the wall were done to get the royal OK. Notice in the group of four robes how Franz marked an X on his choice.

▶ *For more on how Napoleon had an impact on Habsburg Austria, pass through Room 9 and into...*

Room 5

Ponder the ❸ **Cradle of the King of Rome,** once occupied by Napoleon's son, who was born in 1811 and made King of Rome. The little eagle at the foot is symbolically not yet able to fly, but glory-bound. Glory is symbolized by the star, with dad's big *N* raised high. While it's

The crown of Holy Roman Emperor Rudolf II

Napoleon's son's luxurious cradle

fun to think of Napoleon's baby snoozing in here, this was actually a ceremonial "throne bed" that was rarely used.

Napoleon Bonaparte (1769-1821) was a French commoner who rose to power as a charismatic general in the Revolution. While pledging allegiance to democracy, he in fact crowned himself Emperor of France and hobnobbed with Europe's royalty. When his wife Josephine could not bear him a male heir, Napoleon divorced her and married into the Habsburg family.

Portraits show Napoleon and his new bride, Marie Louise, Franz I/II's daughter (and Marie-Antoinette's great-niece). Napoleon gave her a **jewel chest** decorated with the bees of industriousness, his personal emblem. With the birth of the baby King of Rome, Napoleon and Marie Louise were poised to start a new dynasty of European rulers...but then Napoleon met his Waterloo, his son died when he was just 21, and the Habsburgs remained in power.

▶ *Exit to the left of the cradle.*

Miscellaneous Wonders
Room 6
For Divine Right kings, even child-rearing was a sacred ritual that needed elaborate regalia for public ceremonies. The 23-pound ❹ **gold basin and pitcher** were used to baptize noble children, who were dressed in the **baptismal dresses** displayed nearby.

Room 7
These ❺ **jewels** are the true "treasures," a cabinet of wonders used by Habsburgs to impress their relatives (or to hock when funds got

low). The irregularly shaped, 2,680-karat **emerald** is rough-cut, as the cutter wanted to do only the minimum to avoid making a mistake and shattering the giant gem. The helmet-like, jewel-studded **crown** (left wall) was a gift from Muslim Turks supporting a Hungarian king who, as a Protestant, was a thorn in the side of the Catholic Habsburgs (who eventually toppled him).

Room 8

The eight-foot-tall, 500-year-old ➏ **"unicorn horn"** (actually a narwhal tusk), was considered to have magical healing powers bestowed from on high. This one was owned by the Holy Roman Emperor—clearly a divine monarch. The huge **agate bowl,** cut from a single piece, may have been made in ancient Roman times and eventually found its way into the collection of their successors, the Habsburgs. It was thought to be the Holy Grail when it was stolen from Constantinople.

Religious Rooms

After Room 8, you enter several rooms of ➐ **religious objects**—crucifixes, chalices, mini-altarpieces, reliquaries, and bishops' vestments. Like the medieval kings who preceded them, Habsburg rulers mixed the institutions of church and state, so these precious religious accoutrements were also part of their display of secular power.

▶ *Browse these rooms, then backtrack, passing by the Cradle of the King of Rome, and eventually reaching...*

Regalia of the Holy Roman Empire

Room 10

The next few rooms contain some of the oldest and most venerated objects in the Treasury—the robes, crowns, and sacred objects of the Holy Roman Emperor.

The big red-silk and gold-thread ➑ **coronation mantle,** nearly 900 years old, was worn by Holy Roman Emperors when they received their crown. Thousands of tiny white pearls were drilled and threaded for this one garment. Notice the oriental imagery: a palm tree in the center, flanked by lions subduing camels. The hem is written in Arabic (wishing its wearer "great wealth, gifts, and pleasure"). This robe, brought back from the East by Crusaders, gave the Germanic emperors an exotic look that recalled great biblical kings such as Solomon. Many Holy Roman Emperors were crowned by the pope himself. That

New kings were draped in this mantle...

...and crowned with a 10th-century crown.

fact, plus this Eastern-looking mantle, helped put the "Holy" in Holy Roman Emperor.

Room 11

The collection's highlight is the 10th-century ❾ **crown of the Holy Roman Emperor.** It was probably made for Otto I (c. 960), the first king to call himself Holy Roman Emperor.

The Imperial Crown swirls with symbolism "proving" that the emperor was both holy and Roman: The cross on top says the HRE ruled as Christ's representative on earth, and the jeweled arch over the top is reminiscent of the parade helmet of ancient Romans. The jewels themselves allude to the wearer's kinghood in the here and now. Imagine the impression this priceless, glittering crown must have made on the emperor's medieval subjects.

King Solomon's portrait on the crown (to the right of the cross) is Old Testament proof that kings can be wise and good. King David (next panel) is similar proof that they can be just. The crown's eight sides represent the celestial city of Jerusalem's eight gates. The jewels on the front panel symbolize the 12 apostles.

On the forehead of the crown, notice that beneath the cross there's a pale-blue, heart-shaped sapphire. Look a little small for the prime spot? That's because this is a replacement for a long-lost opal said to have had almost mythical, magical powers.

Nearby is the 11th-century **Imperial Cross** that preceded the emperor in ceremonies. Encrusted with jewels, it had a hollow compartment (its core is wood) that carried substantial chunks thought to be from the cross on which Jesus was crucified and the Holy Lance used to pierce his side (both pieces are displayed in the same glass

Charlemagne (Karl der Grosse) and the Holy Roman Empire

The title "Holy Roman Emperor" conveyed three important concepts: **Holy,** meaning the emperor ruled by divine authority (not as a pagan Roman); **Roman,** indicating he was a successor to the ancient Roman Empire; and **Emperor,** meaning he ruled over many different nationalities.

Charlemagne (747-814) briefly united much of Western Europe—that is, the former Roman Empire. On Christmas Eve in the year 800, he was crowned "Roman Emperor" by the pope in St. Peter's Basilica in Rome. After Charlemagne's death, the empire split apart. His successors (who ruled only a portion of Charlemagne's empire) still wanted to envision themselves as inheritors of Charlemagne's greatness. They took to calling themselves Roman Emperors, adding the "Holy" part in the 11th century to emphasize that they ruled by divine authority.

The Holy Roman Emperorship was an elected, not necessarily hereditary, office. Traditionally, the rulers of four important provinces would gather with three powerful archbishops to pick the new ruler, who was usually a Habsburg.

At the empire's peak around 1520, Emperor Charles V ruled from Vienna to Spain, from Holland to Sicily, and from Bohemia to Bolivia in the New World. But throughout much of its existence, the HRE consisted of little more than petty dukes, ruling a loose coalition of independent nobles. It was Voltaire who quipped that the HRE was "neither holy, nor Roman, nor an empire." Napoleon ended the title in 1806. The last Habsburg emperors (including Franz Josef) were merely emperors of Austria.

case). Holy Roman Emperors actually carried the lance into battle in the 10th century. Look behind the cross to see how it was a box that could be clipped open and shut, used for holding holy relics. You can see bits of the "true cross" anywhere, but this is a prime piece—with the actual nail hole.

Another case has additional objects used in the coronation

ceremony: The **orb** (orbs were modeled on late-Roman ceremonial objects, then topped with the cross) and **scepter** (the one with the oak leaves), along with the sword, were carried ahead of the emperor in the procession. In earlier times, these objects were thought to have belonged to Charlemagne himself, the greatest ruler of medieval Europe, but in fact they're mostly from 300 to 400 years later (c. 1200).

Another glass case contains more objects said to belong to Charlemagne. Some of these may be authentic, since they're closer to his era. You'll see the jeweled, purse-like **reliquary of St. Stephen** and the **saber of Charlemagne.** The gold-covered **Book of the Gospels** was the Bible that emperors placed their hands on to swear the oath of office.

Room 12

Now picture all this regalia used together. The ⑩ **Josef II painting** shows the coronation of Maria Theresa's son as Holy Roman Emperor in 1764. Set in a church in Frankfurt (filled with the bigwigs—literally—of the day), Josef is wearing the same crown and royal garb that you've just seen.

Emperors followed the same coronation ritual that originated in the 10th century. The new emperor would don the mantle. The entourage paraded into a church for Mass, led by the religious authorities carrying the Imperial Cross. The emperor placed his hand on the Book of the Gospels and swore his oath. Then he knelt before the three archbishop Electors, who placed the Imperial Crown on his head (sometimes he even traveled to Rome to be crowned by the pope himself). The new emperor rose, accepted the orb and scepter, and—dut dutta dah!—you had a new ruler.

▶ *The tour is over. Pass through Rooms 13-16 to reach the exit, browsing relics, portraits, and objects along the way.*

Kunsthistorisches Museum Tour

The Kunsthistorwhateveritis Museum—let's just say "Kunst" (koonst)—houses the family collection of Austria's luxury-loving Habsburg rulers. Their joie de vivre is reflected in this collection— some of the most beautiful, sexy, and fun art from two centuries (c. 1450-1650). At their peak of power in the 1500s, the Habsburgs ruled Austria, Germany, northern Italy, the Netherlands, and Spain—and you'll see a wide variety of art from all these places and beyond.

The Neo-Renaissance building is a lavish textbook example of Historicism. Despite its palatial feel, it was originally designed for the same purpose it serves today: to showcase its treasures in an inviting space while impressing visitors with the grandeur of the empire.

A statue of Maria Theresa watches over the Kunsthistorisches Museum and its eclectic art collection.

ORIENTATION

Cost: €18, free for those under age 19, €24 combo-ticket includes the Hofburg Treasury.

Hours: Daily 10:00-18:00, Thu until 21:00, closed Mon Sept-May.

Information: +43 1 525 240, www.khm.at.

Getting There: It's on the Ringstrasse at Maria-Theresien-Platz, U: Volkstheater/Museumsplatz (exit toward *Burgring*).

Tours: The excellent €6 audioguide, covering nearly 600 items, is worthwhile if you want an in-depth tour beyond the works described in this chapter.

Cuisine Art: The café is on the first floor.

Starring: The world's best collection of Bruegel, plus Titian, Caravaggio, a Vermeer gem, and Rembrandt self-portraits.

Of the museum's many exhibits, we'll tour only the Picture Gallery (Gemäldegalerie) on the first floor. Italian-Spanish-French art is on one half of the floor, and Northern European art is on the other. On our tour, we'll get a sampling of each. Note that the museum labels the largest rooms in the Picture Gallery with Roman numerals (Saal I, II, III) and the smaller rooms around the perimeter with Arabic (Rooms 1, 2, 3). The museum constantly moves around paintings, so be flexible, pick up the current floor plan in the lobby, and use it to locate the highlights from this tour.

▶ *Climb the main staircase, featuring Antonio Canova's statue of Theseus clubbing a centaur. At the statue, turn 180 degrees and look up, across the atrium, at the small paintings decorating three arches (between the columns). These exquisite works were done in the 1890s by a young Gustav Klimt when the soon-to-be-famous artist was just a decorator for hire. Bear right when you reach Theseus. At the top of the staircase (at the tempting café), look for Saal VII and walk right into the High Renaissance.*

Italian Renaissance

About the year 1500, Italy was in the midst of a 100-year renaissance, or rebirth, of interest in the art and learning of ancient Greece and Rome. In painting, that meant that ordinary humans and Greek gods joined saints and angels as popular subjects.

Canaletto, Habsburg Palaces

In Saal VII, you'll see glimpses of Baroque art, featuring large, colorful

Canova's statue guides you to the paintings.

Canaletto's 1759 take on Schönbrunn Palace

Kunsthistorisches Museum—First Floor

canvases showcasing over-the-top emotions and pudgy, winged babies (the surefire mark of Baroque). Find paintings by **Canaletto** of the former Habsburg palaces—Schönbrunn and Belvedere—one of which also shows the Viennese skyline in the distance.

▶ *Next, move along into Saal VI to find Caravaggio, who shocked the art world with brutally honest reality.*

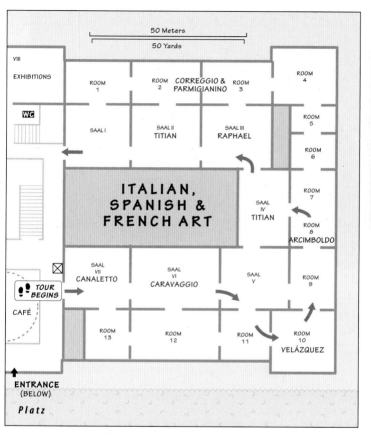

VIII
EXHIBITIONS

WC

ROOM 1

ROOM 2

CORREGGIO & PARMIGIANINO

ROOM 3

ROOM 4

ROOM 5

ROOM 6

SAAL I

SAAL II
TITIAN

SAAL III
RAPHAEL

ROOM 7

ITALIAN, SPANISH & FRENCH ART

SAAL IV
TITIAN

ROOM 8
ARCIMBOLDO

SAAL VII
CANALETTO

SAAL VI
CARAVAGGIO

SAAL V

ROOM 9

TOUR BEGINS

CAFÉ

ROOM 13

ROOM 12

ROOM 11

ROOM 10
VELÁZQUEZ

ENTRANCE (BELOW)

Platz

Caravaggio, *Madonna of the Rosary* and *David with the Head of Goliath*

Caravaggio's *Madonna of the Rosary* (the biggest canvas in the room) may be titled for the Virgin, but the star of the canvas is the plump young Jesus. He casually balances on his mother's knee, one hand rubbing his plump tummy. St. Dominic, to the left of the mother and

Caravaggio paints an unheroic David, stark shadows, and the artist himself in a severed head.

child, distributes rosaries to an imploring crowd (notice their dirty feet—typical of Caravaggio's honest realism).

In *David with the Head of Goliath,* Caravaggio turns a familiar Bible story into a third-degree interrogation as David shoves the dripping head of the slain giant right in our noses. The painting, bled of color, is virtually a black-and-white crime-scene photo—slightly overexposed. Out of the deep darkness shine only a few crucial details. This David is not a heroic Renaissance Man like Michelangelo's famous statue, but a homeless teen that Caravaggio paid to portray God's servant. And the severed head of Goliath is none other than Caravaggio himself, an in-your-face self-portrait.

▶ *Make your way into Room 10, in the corner of the museum.*

Velázquez, Habsburg Family Portraits

When the Habsburgs ruled both Austria and Spain, cousins kept in touch through portraits of themselves and their kids. Diego Velázquez was the greatest of Spain's "photojournalist" painters—heavily influenced by Caravaggio's realism, capturing his subjects without passing judgment, flattering, or glorifying them.

For example, watch little Margarita Habsburg grow up in three different portraits on the same wall, from age two to age nine. Margarita was destined from birth to marry her Austrian cousin, the future Emperor Leopold I. Pictures like these, sent from Spain every few years, let her pen pal/fiancé get to know her.

Also see a portrait of Margarita's little brother, *Philip Prosper*, wearing a dress. Sadly, Philip was a sickly boy who would only live two years longer. The amulets he's wearing were intended to fend off illness.

The kids' oh-so-serious faces, regal poses, and royal trappings are

It's easy to see the Habsburg family resemblance in Velázquez's many royal portraits.

contradicted by their natural precociousness. No wonder Velázquez was so popular.

Also notice that all of these kids are quite, ahem, homely. To understand why, find the portrait of their dad, Philip IV, which shows the defects of royal inbreeding: weepy eyes, an underbite, and a pointed chin (sorry, that pointy mustache doesn't hide anything).

▶ *Continue through the small rooms along the far end of this wing to find (likely in Room 8)...*

Arcimboldo, Portraits of the Seasons

These four cleverly deceptive portraits by the Habsburg court painter, Giuseppe Arcimboldo, depict the four seasons (and elements) as people. For example, take *Summer*—a.k.a. "Fruit Face." With a pickle nose, pear chin, and corn-husk ears, this guy literally is what he eats. Its grotesque weirdness makes it typical of Mannerist art.

▶ *Continue to Saal IV, hung with paintings from floor to ceiling to show how art was displayed in Baroque days by society's elites. Find...*

Titian, *Ecce Homo*

In the long career of Titian the Venetian, he painted portraits, Christian Madonnas, and sexy Venuses with equal ease.

In the large canvas Ecce Homo, a crowd mills about, when suddenly there's a commotion. They nudge each other and start to point. Follow their gaze diagonally up the stairs to a battered figure entering way up in the corner. *"Ecce Homo!"* says Pilate. "Behold the man." And he presents Jesus to the mob. For us, as for the unsympathetic crowd, the humiliated Son of God is not the center of the scene, but almost an afterthought. We'll see a very different Titian canvas a couple of rooms later.

▶ *Continue to Saal III.*

Raphael, *Madonna of the Meadow*

Young Raphael epitomized the spirit of the High Renaissance, combining symmetry, grace, beauty, and emotion. This Madonna is a mountain of motherly love—Mary's head is the summit and her flowing robe is the base—enfolding Baby Jesus and John the Baptist. The geometric perfection, serene landscape, and Mary's adoring face make this a masterpiece of sheer grace—but then you get punched by an

The Habsburgs loved beauty—like Raphael's creamy *Madonna* in a harmonic pyramid pose.

ironic fist: The cross the little tykes play with foreshadows their grue-some deaths.

▶ *Head into Saal II.*

Titian, *Danae*

Titian's *Danae* features a luscious nude reclining in bed, as she's about to be seduced. Zeus, the king of the gods, descends as a shower of gold to consort with her—you can almost see the human form of Zeus within the cloud. Danae is enraptured, opening her legs to receive him, while her servant tries to catch the heavenly spurt with a golden

Titian's *Danae*—a Renaissance centerfold

dish. Danae's rich, luminous flesh is set off by the dark servant at right and the threatening sky above. The white sheets beneath her make her glow even more. This is not just a classic nude—it's a Renaissance Miss August. How could ultraconservative Catholic emperors have tolerated such a downright pagan and erotic painting? Apparently, without a problem.

▶ *Before moving on from the Italian-Spanish-French art section, explore the smaller side rooms. In Rooms 1-3, look for **Correggio's Jupiter and Io,** showing Zeus disguised as a dark cloud seducing a woman, Io. **Parmigianino's Self-Portrait in a Convex Mirror** depicts the artist gazing into a convex mirror and perfectly reproducing the curved reflection on a convex piece of wood. Amazing.*

Exit this wing of the museum via Saal I. Next we'll explore Northern European art.

Northern Art

The "Northern Renaissance," brought on by the economic boom of Dutch and Flemish trading, was more secular and Protestant than

Zeus the seducer moves in like a dark cloud.

One of Arcimboldo's fruity faces

Catholic-funded Italian art. We'll see fewer Madonnas, saints, and Greek gods and more peasants, landscapes, and food. Paintings are smaller and darker, full of down-to-earth objects. Northern artists sweated the details, encouraging the patient viewer to appreciate the beauty in everyday things.

▶ *On your way out of the Italian-Spanish-French wing, drop into Saal VIII (to your right as you leave Saal I), which may hold some must-see paintings (including, possibly, Rubens' portrait of his young bride, described on the next page). To continue to the Northern Art wing, head toward the dome, through the café, and into Saal XV.*

Peter Paul Rubens

Rubens' work runs the gamut, from realistic portraits to lounging nudes, from Greek myths to altarpieces, from pious devotion to violent sex.

But can we be sure it's Baroque? Ah yes, I'm sure you'll find a pudgy, winged baby somewhere, hovering in the heavens. Take the large *Ildefonso Altarpiece* (likely in Saal XIII), a rare canvas done entirely in Rubens' hand, where a glorious Mary appears—with her entourage of darling PWBs—to reward the grateful Spanish St. Ildefonso with a chasuble (priest's smock).

Look for Rubens' *Self-Portrait* (likely Room 20) and admire the darling of Catholic-dominated Flanders (northern Belgium) in his

Hélène Fourment, teenage wife...   ...of middle-aged Rubens

prime: famous, wealthy, well-traveled, the friend of kings and princes, an artist, diplomat, man about town, and—obviously—confident.

The 53-year-old Rubens married Hélène Fourment, a dimpled girl of 16, whose portrait you may find in Saal VIII. Notice how she pulls the fur around her ample flesh, simultaneously covering herself and exalting her charms. Rubens called this painting *The Little Fur*—and used the same name for his young bride. Hmm.

How could Rubens paint all these enormous canvases in one lifetime? He had help. He ran a busy studio with about 60 artists. Rubens generally painted a small model "cartoon" (you can see several here) from which his team of artists would paint the big canvas. He'd then amp up their work with what he called "the fury of the brush" and it was shipped out...another Rubens masterpiece. For example, the giant canvas *The Miracles of St. Ignatius of Loyola* (likely in Saal XIV) was painted partly by assistants, guided by Rubens' sketches.

▶ *Explore the world of Rubens and the rooms on the far end. Then duck into Saal XII to see a little jewel of a canvas by Vermeer.*

Jan Vermeer

In his small canvases, the Dutch painter Jan Vermeer quiets the world down to where we can hear our own heartbeat, letting us appreciate the beauty in common things.

The curtain opens and we see *The Art of Painting,* a behind-the-scenes look at Vermeer at work. He's painting a model dressed in blue, starting with her laurel-leaf headdress. The studio is its own dollhouse world framed by a chair in the foreground and the wall in back. Then Vermeer fills this space with the few gems he wants us to focus on—the chandelier, the map, the painter's costume. Everything is lit

Rubens' huge canvases dwarf visitors.

by a crystal-clear light, letting us see these everyday items with fresh eyes.

The painting is also called *The Allegory of Painting*. The model has the laurel leaves, trumpet, and book that symbolize the muse of history and fame. The artist—his back to the public—earnestly tries to capture fleeting fame with a small sheet of canvas.

▶ *Also in Saal XII, look for dark, brooding works by...*

Rembrandt van Rijn

Rembrandt became wealthy by painting portraits of Holland's up-wardly mobile businessmen, but his greatest subject was himself. In his *Large Self-Portrait* we see the hands-on-hips, defiant, open-stance determination of a man who will do what he wants, and if people don't like it, tough.

In typical Rembrandt style, most of the canvas is a dark, smudgy brown, with only the side of his face glowing from the darkness. (Remember Caravaggio? Rembrandt did.) Unfortunately, the year this was painted, Rembrandt's fortunes changed.

Vermeer's *Art of Painting*—The curtain opens, and we see the diligent genius at work.

Looking at the *Small Self-Portrait* from 1657, consider Rembrandt's last years. His wife died, his children died young, and commissions for paintings dried up as his style veered from the popular style of the day. He had to auction off paintings to pay his debts, and he died a poor man. Rembrandt's numerous self-portraits painted from youth until old age show a man always changing—from wide-eyed youth to successful portraitist to this disillusioned, but still defiant, old man.

▶ *Nearby, Saal X contains the largest collection of Bruegels in captivity. Linger. If you like it, linger longer.*

Pieter Bruegel the Elder

The undisputed master of the slice-of-life village scene was Pieter Bruegel the Elder (c. 1525-1569)—think of him as the Norman Rockwell of the 16th century. His name (pronounced "BROY-gull") is sometimes spelled *Brueghel*. Don't confuse Pieter Bruegel the Elder with his sons, Pieter Brueghel the Younger and Jan Brueghel, who added luster and an "h" to the family name (and whose works are also displayed in the Kunst). Despite his many rural paintings, Bruegel was a cultivated

Rembrandt—the master of self-portraits…   …each one showing a subtle new emotion

urbanite who liked to wear peasants' clothing to observe country folk at play. He celebrated their simple life, but he also skewered their weaknesses—not to single them out as hicks, but as universal examples of human folly. About a quarter of all known Bruegel paintings are gathered in this exciting room.

The Peasant Wedding, Bruegel's most famous work, is less about the wedding than the food. It's a farmers' feeding frenzy, as the barnful of wedding guests scramble to get their share of free eats. Two men bring in the next course, a tray of fresh porridge. The bagpiper pauses to check it out. A guy grabs bowls and passes them down the table, taking our attention with them. Everyone's going at it, including a kid in an oversized red cap who licks the bowl with his fingers. In the middle of it all, look who's been completely forgotten—the demure bride sitting in front of the blue-green cloth. According to Flemish tradition, the bride was not allowed to speak or eat at the party, and the groom was not in attendance at all. (Also check out the guy carrying the front end of the food tray—is he stepping forward with his right leg, or with his left, or with…all three?)

Speaking of two left feet, Bruegel's *Peasant Dance* shows a celebration at the consecration of a village church. Peasants happily clog to the tune of a lone bagpiper, who wails away while his pit crew keeps him lubed with wine. Notice the overexuberant guy in the green hat on the left, who accidentally smacks his buddy in the face. As with his other peasant paintings, Bruegel captures the warts-and-all scene accurately—it's neither romanticized nor patronizing.

Bruegel's peasants dance, eat, drink, and sing in the Kunst's collection—the world's largest.

Find several Bruegel landscape paintings. These are part of an original series of six "calendar" paintings. *Gloomy Day* opens the cycle, as winter turns to spring...slowly. The snow has melted, flooding the distant river. The trees are still leafless, and the villagers stir, cutting wood and mending fences. We skip ahead to autumn in The Return of the Herd—still sunny, but winter's storms are fast approaching. Finally, in *Hunters in Snow,* it's the dead of winter, and three dog-tired hunters with their tired dogs trudge along with only a single fox to show for their efforts. As they crest the hill, the grove of bare trees opens to a breathtaking view—they're almost home, where they can join their mates playing hockey. Birds soar like the hunters' rising spirits—emerging from winter's work and looking ahead to a new year.

The Tower of Babel, modeled after Rome's Colosseum, stretches into the clouds, towering over the village. Impressive as it looks, on closer inspection the tower is crooked—destined eventually to tumble onto the village. Even so, the king (in the foreground) demands further work.

Bruegel's party extends beyond the frame.

A quiet scene of country life

▶ *For an unforgettable finale, return to the entry, taking the stairs back to the ground level. Take the stairs to the right to enter the Kunstkammer.*

Rest of the Kunst

The *Kunstkammer* shows off the personal collection of *objets d'art* of the House of Habsburg. Amassed by 17 emperors over the centuries, the *Kunstkammer* ("art cabinet") is a dazzling display of 2,000 ancient treasures, medieval curios, and jeweled wonders collected from the year 800 to 1891. The U-shaped gallery is laid out chronologically, beautifully lit, and thoughtfully described in English.

The highlight is at the end of the first long hall (on the left in Room XXIX): Benvenuto Cellini's famous golden salt cellar. It was pounded out of a sheet of gold in 1543 by the renowned Florentine goldsmith. Featuring gods of the sea and the earth with symbols of winds and seasons all around, it takes salting and peppering your food to Habsburg heights.

Budget time for Bruegel's colorful canvases.

Kick back and enjoy this tiny salt cellar.

Schönbrunn Palace Tour

Among Europe's palaces, only Schönbrunn rivals Versailles. This former summer residence of the Habsburgs is big, with more than 300 rooms in the main building alone. But don't worry—only 40 rooms are shown to the public. Of the plethora of sights at the vast complex, the highlight is a tour of the palace's ▲▲▲ Imperial Apartments—the chandeliered rooms where the Habsburg nobles lived. You can also stroll the ▲▲ gardens, tour the Imperial Carriage Museum, and visit a handful of lesser sights nearby.

Cost: Visits to the palace are by timed-entry tour (book in advance). There are two tour options for the Imperial Apartments (both come with audioguides). The best is the 40-room **Grand Tour,** which includes both the rooms of Franz Josef and Sisi, as well as the more impressive Rococo rooms of Maria Theresa (€26, 50 minutes, covered by Sisi Ticket). The **Imperial Tour** covers only the less-interesting first 22 rooms (€22, 35 minutes).

If venturing beyond the apartments, consider the **Classic Pass** combo-ticket, which includes the Grand Tour, as well as the Gloriette viewing terrace, maze, orangery, and privy garden (€31, available April-Oct only).

Hours: Imperial Apartments open daily 9:00-17:00, July-Aug until 17:30; gardens generally open 6:30-20:00. The palace is busiest from 9:00 to 12:00, and crowds start to subside after 14:00.

Information: +43 1 811 130, www.schoenbrunn.at.

Advance Tickets Recommended: To get right in, book your entry time in advance online. Otherwise, you'll likely have to stand in line at the ticket desk, and wait again for your assigned entry time—which could be hours later. Those with a Sisi Ticket can enter without a reserved entry time (buy your Sisi Ticket online or at the Imperial Furniture Museum—see page 126 for details).

If you don't have a reservation, come early or late and use one of the ticket machines.

Getting There: Schönbrunn is an easy 10-minute subway ride from downtown. Take U-4 from Karlsplatz to Schönbrunn (direction: Hütteldorf) and follow signs for *Schloss Schönbrunn*. Exit bearing right, then cross the busy road and continue to the right, to the far, far end of the long yellow building.

Length of This Tour: Allow at least three hours (including transit time). The palace itself is sprawling and can be mobbed. After viewing the Imperial Apartments, wander the gardens (most of which are free).

THE TOUR BEGINS

In the 1500s, the Habsburgs built a small hunting lodge near a beautiful spring *(schön-brunn),* and for the next three centuries, they made it their summer getaway from stuffy Vienna. The palace's exterior (late-1600s) is Baroque, but the interior was finished under Maria Theresa (mid-1700s) in let-them-eat-cake Rococo. As with the similar apartments at the Hofburg (the Habsburgs' winter home), these apartments give you a sense of the quirky, larger-than-life personalities who lived here. It's the place where Maria Theresa raised her brood of 16 kids... where six-year-old Mozart played his first big gig...and where Maria Theresa's great-great-grandson Franz Josef (r. 1848-1916) tried to please his self-absorbed wife Elisabeth, a.k.a. Sisi.

Your tour of the apartments, accompanied by an audioguide, follows a clearly signed one-way route. Think of the following minitour as a series of breadcrumbs, leading you along while the audioguide fills in the details.

▶ *With your ticket in hand, approach the palace. Follow signs to the entrance gate stamped on your ticket. When your entry time arrives, politely push your way through the milling crowds to get to the turnstiles. If you're doing the Grand Tour, keep your ticket handy as you'll need it again.*

The backyard of the emperors' summer palace, with the Gloriette in the distance.

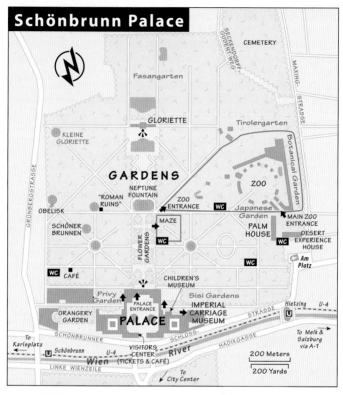

Schönbrunn Palace

Imperial Apartments

Begin in the **guards' room,** where jauntily dressed mannequins of Franz Josef's bodyguards introduce you to his luxurious world. Continue through the Billiard Room to the **Walnut Room.** Wow. Rococo-style wood paneling and gilding decorate this room where Franz Josef—a hard-working modern monarch—received official visitors. Nearby is the **study**—Franz Josef (see his mustachioed portrait) worked at this desk, sometimes joined by his beautiful, brown-haired wife Sisi (see her portrait). In the **bedchamber,** a praying stool, iron bed, and little toilet all attest to Franz Josef's spartan lifestyle (though the paintings here remind us of the grand scale of his palace).

▶ *As you turn the corner, you enter...*

Empress Sisi's Study and Dressing Room

See her portrait in a black dress, as well as a reconstruction of the spiral staircase that once led down to her apartments. The long-haired mannequin and makeup jars in the dressing room indicate how obsessive Sisi was about her looks.

▶ *Pass through this room to reach...*

Franz Josef's and Sisi's Bedroom

The huge wood-carved double bed suggests marital bliss, but the bed is not authentic—and as for the bliss, history suggests otherwise.

Follow along to the **dining room.** The whole family ate here at the huge table; today it's set with dinnerware owned by Maria Theresa and Sisi. Next is the **children's room,** with portraits of Maria Theresa (on the easel) and some of her 11 (similar-looking) daughters. The bathroom was installed for the last Habsburg empress, Zita.

▶ *Turning the corner, pass through two rooms, until you reach the...*

Many of Schönbrunn's rooms have period furniture, like the bedroom of Franz Josef and Sisi.

Hall of Mirrors

In this room, six-year-old Mozart performed for Maria Theresa and her family (1762). He amazed them by playing without being able to see the keys, he jumped playfully into the empress' lap, and he even asked six-year-old Marie-Antoinette to marry him.

▶ *Pass through the next room, which leads to the large, breathtaking, white-and-gold...*

Great Gallery

Imagine the parties they had here: waltzers spinning across the floor, lit by chandeliers reflecting off the mirrors, beneath stunning ceiling frescoes—and outside, views of the gardens and the Gloriette monument (described later). When WWII bombs rained on Vienna, the palace was largely spared. It took only one direct hit—crashing through this ballroom—but thankfully, that bomb was a dud. In 1961, President Kennedy and Soviet Premier Khrushchev met here.

▶ *Pass through the final three rooms (pausing at a painting of Maria Theresa riding a Lipizzaner horse) until you reach the...*

The lavishly stuccoed Great Gallery was the palace's main party room.

Hall of Ceremonies

Wedding receptions were held here, beneath a regal portrait of Maria Theresa in a pink lace dress.

▶ *As you prepare to leave this room, look to the left of the doorway (to the right of Maria Theresa) to find a crowded painting with (supposedly) the child Mozart (behind Plexiglas, sitting next to a priest in gray). If you've bought the Grand Tour ticket, continue on to reach...*

More Fancy Rooms

It was in the **Blue Chinese Salon,** in 1918, that the last Habsburg emperor Karl I made the decision to relinquish power, marking the end of more than six centuries of Habsburg rule. Up next, the black-lacquer **Vieux-Laque Room** was remodeled by Maria Theresa as a memorial to her beloved husband who died unexpectedly. Continue to the **Napoleon Room.** When Napoleon conquered Austria, he took over Schönbrunn and made this his bedroom. He dumped Josephine and took a Habsburg princess as his bride, and they had a son (cutely pictured holding a wreath of flowers).

▶ *Turn the corner through the Porcelain Room and enter the stunning...*

SCHÖNBRUNN PALACE TOUR

It was Maria Theresa (seated at right) who made the palace interior the wonder it is today.

Millions Room

Admire the rosewood paneling inset with little painted scenes, and see how the mirrors reflect to infinity.

▶ *We're nearing the end. Pass through three more (admittedly gorgeous) rooms, and turn the corner into the...*

Rich Bedchamber

This darkened room has what may have been Maria Theresa's wedding bed, where she and her husband Franz produced 16 children. Then comes their **study,** with a fitting end to this palace tour—a painting showing the happy couple who left their mark all over Schönbrunn. Maria Theresa and Franz are surrounded by their brood. Imagine these kids growing up here, riding horses, frolicking in the gardens, and preparing to marry fellow royals in order to bring peace and prosperity to the happy house of Habsburg.

Palace Gardens

The large, manicured grounds fill the palace's backyard, dominated by a hill-topping monument called the Gloriette, a purely decorative monument celebrating an obscure Austrian military victory. It's a delightful, sprawling place to wander—especially on a sunny day. You can spend hours here, enjoying the views and the people-watching. And most of the park is free, as it has been for centuries (open daily sunrise to dusk, entrance on either side of the palace). Note that some specialty features in the gardens charge admission but are included in the Classic Pass described earlier (under "Cost").

Next door to the palace grounds is the world's oldest zoo (*Tiergarten*), built in 1752 by Maria Theresa's husband for the entertainment and education of the court. Today, it's a modern A (anteater) to Z (zebra) menagerie that's especially appealing to families (adults-€24, kids-€14, daily 9:00-18:30, closes earlier off-season, www.zoovienna.at). The Schönbrunn Imperial Carriage Museum is a 19th-century traffic jam of 50 impressive royal carriages and sleighs (€12, daily 9:00-17:00, shorter hours off-season, audioguide-€2, 200 yards from palace, walk through right arch as you face palace, +43 1 525 242 500, www.kaiserliche-wagenburg.at).

Sights

For centuries, Vienna has been an epicenter of European culture: fine music, exquisite art, dress-up balls, enlightened city planning, and cutting-edge science. As a result, today's Vienna has a dizzying number of sights and museums, which cover the city's rich heritage and vivid history. Just perusing the list on a tourist map can be overwhelming. To get you started, I've selected the sights that are most essential, rewarding, and user-friendly, and arranged them by neighborhood for handy sightseeing.

When you see a 📖 in a listing, it means the sight is covered in greater detail in my Vienna City Walk or one of my self-guided tours. A 🎧 means the walk or tour is also available as a free audio tour (via my Rick Steves Audio Europe app—see page 11).

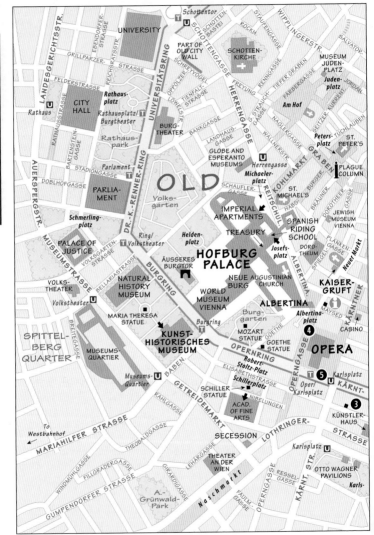

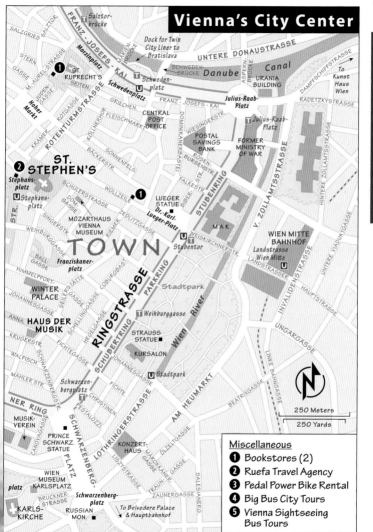

Vienna's City Center

Miscellaneous

1. Bookstores (2)
2. Ruefa Travel Agency
3. Pedal Power Bike Rental
4. Big Bus City Tours
5. Vienna Sightseeing Bus Tours

250 Meters

250 Yards

SIGHTSEEING PASSES AND COMBO-TICKETS

Avid sightseers should consider a pass or combo-ticket, but do the math first. Add up the cost of all the sights you think you'll see, then consider whether you'd like to use the hop-on, hop-off bus to get around (included with the Vienna Pass). If you prefer to walk or take public transportation, you may be better off with one or more of the combo-tickets described below.

Passes: The **Vienna Pass** is likely not worthwhile for most travelers unless you plan to use hop-on, hop-off tour buses (€85/1 day, €119/2 days, €149/3 days; www.viennapass.com).

Combo-Tickets: The €40 **Sisi Ticket** covers the Hofburg Imperial Apartments (with its Sisi Museum and Silver Collection—must see both on the same day), Schönbrunn Palace's Grand Tour, and the Vienna Furniture Museum. At Schönbrunn, the ticket lets you enter the palace immediately, without a reserved entry time. Buy your Sisi Ticket in advance online (www.schoenbrunn.at or www.sisimuseum-hofburg.at) or at the Vienna Furniture Museum, where lines are shorter.

If you're seeing the **Hofburg Treasury** (royal regalia and crown jewels) and the **Kunsthistorisches** (world-class art collection), the €24 combo-ticket saves you money.

The **Haus der Musik** (mod museum with interactive exhibits) has a combo deal with **Mozarthaus Vienna** (exhibits and artifacts about the great composer) for €20—saving a few euros for music lovers (though the Mozarthaus will likely disappoint all but the most diehard Mozart fans).

HOFBURG PALACE SIGHTS

The imposing Imperial Palace, with 640 years of architecture, art, and history, demands your attention. The winter residence of the Habsburg rulers until 1918, the Hofburg is still home to the Austrian president's office, 5,000 government workers, and several important museums. Focus on three sights: the Imperial Apartments, the Treasury, and the museums in the World Museum Vienna. With more time, consider the Hofburg's many other sights, including the Spanish Riding School, the Augustinian Church, the Albertina Museum, and Kaisergruft, all described next. On Sunday mornings in season, the Hofburg comes alive

The Hofburg has many sights and museums. Follow me to the Vienna Boys' Choir!

with three wonderful events: the Vienna Boys' Choir (9:15; see page 155), a Spanish Riding School performance (11:00; described later), and the Augustinian Church Mass (11:00; described later).

See the 📖 Hofburg Imperial Apartments Tour chapter and the 📖 Hofburg Treasury Tour chapter

▲▲World Museum Vienna (Weltmuseum Wien)

The World Museum Vienna houses several museums: They're all part of one grand building and covered by one ticket. The World Museum is technically only the mezzanine level, which houses an expansive ethnology collection (displaying souvenirs from Habsburg expeditions around the world). The same ticket also grants you access to the Imperial Armory (with a killer collection of medieval weapons) and the impressive Collection of Historic Musical Instruments (including Beethoven's supposed clarinet and a strange keyboard perhaps played by Mozart). An added bonus of the World Museum is a chance to wander among the royal Habsburg halls, stairways, and painted ceilings virtually alone.

▶ €16, worthwhile audioguide-€5; Thu-Mon 10:00-18:00, Tue until 21:00, closed Wed; +43 1 534 30 5052, www.weltmuseumwien.at.

▲Spanish Riding School (Spanische Hofreitschule)

The regal Lipizzaner stallions prance to music under chandeliers in a stately 300-year-old Baroque hall. Since the 1500s, these horses have been bred by the Habsburgs to create an intelligent breed with a noble gait and Baroque profile. They're born black, fade to gray, and don't turn into their trademark white until adulthood.

Seeing the Horses and Buying Tickets: The school offers three ways to see the horses—performances, morning exercises, and guided tours of the stables (check the events list on the school's **website** at www.srs.at). You can purchase tickets online or at the **box office** (opens at 9:00, located inside the Hofburg—go through the main Hofburg entryway from Michaelerplatz, then turn left into the first passage, +43 1 533 9031).

To **see the horses for free,** look for the covered passageway across from Josefsplatz. There's a big window from where you can usually see the horses poking their heads out of their stalls.

Performances: The Lipizzaner stallions put on great 80-minute performances nearly year-round. With just a few rows of seats and close-up standing-room spots, there's not a bad view in the house (seats about €50-160, standing room about €25, prices vary depending on the show; Feb-mid-June and mid-Aug-Dec usually Sat-Sun at 11:00, no shows Jan and mid-June-mid-Aug).

Morning Exercises: For a more casual experience, morning exercises with music take place on weekday mornings in the same hall and are open to the public. Tourists line up early at Josefsplatz (the large courtyard between Michaelerplatz and Albertinaplatz). Tuesdays are busiest (€15; tickets may be available at the door in high season, but best to buy in advance online or at the box office; generally Tue-Fri 10:00-11:00, no exercises July-mid-Aug).

Guided Tours: One-hour guided tours of the school and stables in English are given almost every afternoon year-round (€19; tours usually daily at 13:00, 14:00, 15:00, and 16:00; reserve ahead by emailing office@srs.at or calling the box office).

▲Augustinian Church (Augustinerkirche)

Built into the Hofburg, this is the Gothic and Neo-Gothic church where the Habsburgs got married. Today, the royal hearts are in the church vault.

Inside (above the altar on the right), notice the windows from which royals witnessed the Mass in private. Look back at what's considered the finest pipe organ in Vienna. From the front, circle back to the right, walking up the aisle along the right wall. A wooden door leads to a crypt with the hearts of 54 Habsburg nobles in urns (viewable by German tour only, €3, after Sunday Mass at about 12:45). Don't miss the exquisite, pyramid-shaped memorial (by the Italian sculptor Antonio Canova) to Maria Theresa's favorite daughter, Maria Christina. The church's 11:00 Sunday Mass is a hit with music lovers.

It's often with an orchestra accompanying the choir—typically you'll hear one of Mozart's or Haydn's many short Masses.

▶ *Free, open long hours daily; Augustinerstrasse 3.*

▲▲Albertina Museum

This impressive museum has three highlights: the imposing state rooms of the former palace, noteworthy collections of classic modernist paintings and European graphic arts (sketches, etching, watercolors—especially Dürer), and excellent temporary exhibits. The building, at the southern tip of the Hofburg complex (near the opera), was the residence of Maria Theresa's favorite daughter, Maria Christina. Her husband, Albert of Saxony, was a great collector of original drawings and prints, which he amassed to cover all the important art movements from the late Middle Ages until the early 19th century (including prized works by Dürer, Rembrandt, and Rubens).

State Rooms (level 1): Wander freely under chandeliers and across parquet floors through a handful of rooms of 18th-century imperial splendor. Most impressive is the large Hall of Muses (in pastel yellow), lined with statues of the graceful demi-goddesses (plus Apollo) who inspire the arts.

Batliner Collection (level 2): This manageable collection sweeps you quickly through modern art history, featuring minor works by major artists. You'll see classic Impressionism: Monet's water lilies, Degas' dancers, and Renoir's cute little girls. The next rooms illustrate how art transitioned from Impressionism to abstraction: the bright colors of Fauvism, and the thick paint and grotesque figures of Expressionism.

The Picasso room has canvases from various periods of his life:

Ogle the Albertina's art collection...

...and the splendor of its state rooms.

early Cubist experiments, portraits of the women in his life, and exuberant, colorful works from his last years on the sunny Riviera. Surrealism, paintings by Joan Miró, and big Abstract Expressionist canvases bring art up to the cusp of the 21st century.

▶ €19; daily 10:00-18:00, Wed and Fri until 21:00; overlooking Albertinaplatz across from the TI and opera house, +43 1 534 830, www. albertina.at.

CHURCH CRYPTS NEAR THE HOFBURG

Two churches near the Hofburg offer starkly different looks at dearly departed Viennese: the Habsburg coffins in the Kaisergruft and the commoners' graves in St. Michael's Church.

▲▲Kaisergruft (Imperial Crypt)

Visiting the imperial remains of the Habsburg family is not as easy as you might imagine. These original organ donors left their bodies—about 150 in all—in the unassuming Kaisergruft, their hearts in the Augustinian Church, and their entrails in the crypt below St. Stephen's Cathedral.

Descend into a crypt full of gray metal tombs. Start up the path, through tombs ranging from simple caskets to increasingly big monuments, to the massive pewter tomb of **Maria Theresa** under the dome. The only female Habsburg monarch, her 40-year reign was enlightened and progressive. She and her husband, **Franz I,** recline atop their fancy coffin, gazing into each other's eyes as a cherub crowns them with glory. At his parents' feet lies **Josef II,** the patron of Mozart and Beethoven.

Continuing to the right of Maria Theresa's tomb, you'll pass the tombs of **Franz II** and his son **Ferdinand I.** These two 19th-century rulers were forced to relinquish some of the Habsburg power in the face of Napoleon's armies and democratic revolutions.

Head on through the next room and down three steps to a room with the appropriately austere military tomb of the long-reigning **Franz Josef,** his wife, **Elisabeth**—a.k.a. Sisi, and their son Crown Prince Rudolf. In the final room find **Karl I** (see his bust, not a tomb), the last of the Habsburg rulers, who was deposed in 1918. When his

Maria Theresa and her husband relax atop their enormous tomb in the Kaisergruft.

son, Crown Prince **Otto,** was laid to rest here in 2011, it was probably the last great Old Regime event in European history.

▶ *€8, daily 10:00-18:00, free map includes Habsburg family tree and a chart locating each coffin, crypt is in the Capuchin Church at Tegetthoffstrasse 2 at Neuer Markt; +43 1 512 685 388.*

▲St. Michael's Church Crypt (Michaelerkirche)

St. Michael's Church offers a striking contrast to the imperial crypt. Tours take visitors underground to see a typical church crypt, filled with the rotting wooden coffins of well-to-do commoners. You'll meet 18th-century mummies in their original clothes—one wearing lederhosen and a wig; another clutching a cross and wearing high heels painted with flowers.

▶ *€8 for 45-minute tour (crypt only accessible by tour), tours run Fri-Sat only, check website to confirm schedule and language—tours may be in German only, wait at church entrance at the sign advertising the tour and pay the guide directly, +43 650 533 8003, www.michaelerkirche.at.*

MORE SIGHTS WITHIN THE RING

▲▲▲St. Stephen's Cathedral (Stephansdom)

This massive Gothic church with the skyscraping spire sits at the center of Vienna. Its highlights are the impressive exterior, the view from the top of the south tower, a carved pulpit, and a handful of quirky sights associated with Mozart and the Habsburg rulers.

　　📖 See the St. Stephen's Cathedral Tour chapter or 🎧 download my free audio tour.

▲▲▲Vienna State Opera (Wiener Staatsoper)

Vienna remains one of the world's great cities for classical music, and this building still belts out some of the finest opera, both classic and cutting-edge. The only way to see the opera house interior (besides attending a performance—see the Activities chapter) is with a guided 40-minute tour. You'll see the opulent halls where operagoers gather at intermission, enjoying elaborate spaces with coffered ceilings, gold trim, and iron-work lamps. The highlight is the 2,000-seat theater itself—where the main floor is ringed by box seating, under a huge sugar-doughnut chandelier.

▶ *€13, tour schedule varies depending on rehearsals and performances—generally more tours in the afternoon and in July-Aug; reserve your spot online or risk it and show up at the tour entrance 30 minutes in advance; current month's tour schedule posted online, at the tour entrance (on Operngasse), and at the box office (on Kärntner Strasse); +43 1 514 444 2250, www.wiener-staatsoper.at/en/staatsoper/guided-tours.*

▲▲Haus der Musik

Vienna's "House of Music" is a fun and interactive experience that celebrates this hometown forte. The museum, spread over several floors and well-described in English, is unique for its effective use of touchscreen computers and headphones to explore the physics of sound. One floor is dedicated to the heavyweight Viennese composers (Mozart, Beethoven, and company) who virtually created classical music as we know it. It's open late and is so interactive, relaxing, and fun that it can be considered an activity more than a sight—an evening of joy for music lovers.

▶ *€16, half-price after 20:00, €20 combo-ticket with Mozarthaus, daily 10:00-22:00, two blocks from the opera house at Seilerstätte 30, +43 1 513 4850, www.hausdermusik.com.*

Tour the opera house, no reservation needed.

Conduct a virtual band at Haus der Musik.

▲St. Peter's Church (Peterskirche)

Baroque Vienna is at its best in this architectural gem, tucked away a few steps from the Graben. Admire the rose-and-gold, oval-shaped Baroque interior, topped with a ceiling fresco of Mary kneeling to be crowned by Jesus and the Father, while the dove of the Holy Spirit floats way up in the lantern. The church's sumptuous elements—especially the organ, altar painting, pulpit, and coat of arms of church founder Leopold I—make St. Peter's one of the city's most beautiful and ornate churches.

▶ *Free, Mon-Fri 8:00-19:00, Sat-Sun from 9:00, free organ concerts daily at 15:00, just off the Graben between the Plague Monument and Kohlmarkt, +43 1 533 6433, www.peterskirche.at.*

Mozarthaus Vienna Museum

In September 1784, 27-year-old Wolfgang Amadeus Mozart moved into this spacious apartment with his wife, Constanze, and their week-old son Karl. For the next three years, this was the epicenter of Viennese high life. It was here that Mozart wrote *Marriage of Figaro* and *Don Giovanni* and established himself as the toast of Vienna. Today, the actual apartments are pretty boring (mostly bare rooms), but the museum does flesh out Mozart's Vienna years with paintings, videos, and a few period pieces.

▶ *€12, includes audioguide, €20 combo-ticket with Haus der Musik; Tue-Sun 10:00-18:00, closed Mon; a block behind the cathedral, go through arcade at #5a and walk 50 yards to Domgasse 5, +43 1 512 1791, www.mozarthausvienna.at.*

MUSEUM DISTRICT

▲▲▲Kunsthistorisches Museum

This exciting museum, across the Ring from the Hofburg Palace, show-cases the grandeur and opulence of the Habsburgs' collected artwork in a grand building. You'll find world-class European masterpieces galore (including canvases by Raphael, Caravaggio, Velázquez, Rubens, Vermeer, Rembrandt, and a particularly exquisite roomful of Bruegels).

📖 See the Kunsthistorisches Museum Tour chapter.

▲▲Natural History Museum (Naturhistorisches Museum)

The twin building facing the Kunsthistorisches Museum still serves the exact purpose for which it was built: to show off the Habsburgs' vast collection of plant, animal, and mineral specimens and artifacts. It's grown to become an exceptionally well-organized and enjoyable catalogue of the natural world, with 20 million objects, including moon rocks, dinosaur stuff, and the fist-sized *Venus of Willendorf* (at 25,000 years old, the world's oldest sex symbol). Even though the museum has kept its old-school charm, nearly everything on display is presented and described well enough to engage any visitor.

▶ *€14; Thu-Mon 9:00-18:30, Wed until 21:00, closed Tue; €6 audioguide ("Top 100") isn't necessary but can help you hit the highlights; on the Ringstrasse at Maria-Theresien-Platz, U: Volkstheater/Museums-platz, +43 1 521 770, www.nhm-wien.ac.at.*

MuseumsQuartier

The vast grounds of the former imperial stables now corral a cutting-edge cultural center for contemporary arts and design. Among several

Tiny statue—older than the pyramids

MuseumsQuartier: Fine art and ambience

impressive museums, the best are the Leopold Museum (Egon Schiele, Gustav Klimt, and Oskar Kokoschka) and the Museum of Modern Art (a.k.a. MUMOK, with 20th-century "classics" like Klee and Picasso). For many, the MuseumsQuartier is most enjoyable as a spot to gather in the evening for a light, fun meal, cocktails, and people-watching.

The charming **Spittelberg** neighborhood, just beyond the MuseumsQuartier, hosts a range of pleasant eateries, including a lovely wine garden just a five-minute walk away (see page 179).

▶ *The main entrance/visitors center is at Museumsplatz 1. Check out the museums at their websites (www.leopoldmuseum.org, www.mumok.at).*

SIGHTS

KARLSPLATZ AND NEARBY

These sights cluster around Karlsplatz, just southeast of the Ringstrasse (the Karlsplatz U-Bahn station, which spans a huge area underground—from the opera, to Karlsplatz, to the Naschmarkt—can be accessed at the opera house). If you're walking from central Vienna, use the station entrance at the opera house and follow the passageways to avoid crossing busy boulevards.

The picnic-friendly square, with its Henry Moore sculpture in the pond, faces the imposing facade of Vienna's Technical University. The small green, white, and gold pavilions that line the street across the square were designed by the Modernist architect **Otto Wagner.** One of the pavilions has a sweet little exhibit on Wagner that illustrates the Art Nouveau lifestyle around 1900.

Art Nouveau pavilion by Otto Wagner

The Karlskirche, with its 235-foot dome

▲**Karlskirche (St. Charles Church)**

This "votive church," with its massive dome, was proposed by Emperor Charles VI and dedicated to his patron saint, St. Charles Borromeo, in 1713 when an epidemic spared Vienna. The church offers some over-the-top Baroque designs, with a unique combination of columns (showing scenes from Borromeo's life), a classic pediment, an elliptical dome, and a terrific close-up look at its colorful 13,500-square-foot fresco, thanks to a construction elevator that's open to the public. The entry fee is steep, but worth it if you visit the dome—but skip it if you're even slightly afraid of heights.

▶ *€8, Mon-Sat 9:00-18:00, Sun 11:00-19:00, dome elevator runs until 17:30, pick up the free info booklet, www.karlskirche.at. There are often classical music concerts performed here on period instruments (usually Thu-Sat, www.concert-vienna.info).*

▲**Academy of Fine Arts Painting Gallery**
(Akademie der Bildenden Künste Gemäldegalerie)

Vienna's art academy has a small but impressive collection of paintings to inspire and instruct its students. The gallery rotates temporary exhibits—everything from the masters to modern art—to illustrate

Among the Academy of Fine Arts' impressive collection of paintings is Bosch's surreal triptych.

contemporary themes. The highlights—a triptych by the master of medieval surrealism, Hieronymus Bosch, and works by Guardi, Titian, Rubens, and Van Dyck—are generally featured in the rotating themed exhibits.

▶ *€9, Tue-Sun 10:00-18:00, closed Mon, three blocks from the opera house at Schillerplatz 3, +43 1 588 162 201, www.kunstsammlungenakademie.at.*

▲The Secession

This little building was created by the Vienna Secession movement, a group of nonconformist artists led by Gustav Klimt, Otto Wagner, and friends (see the sidebar). Having turned their backs on the stuffy official art academy, the Secessionists used the building to display their radical art. The stylized trees carved into the exterior walls and the building's bushy "golden cabbage" rooftop are symbolic of a cycle of renewal. Today, the Secession continues to showcase contemporary cutting-edge art, and it preserves Gustav Klimt's famous *Beethoven Frieze*. A masterpiece of Viennese Art Nouveau (and inspired by Ludwig van Beethoven's *Ninth Symphony*), this 105-foot-long fresco was the multimedia centerpiece of a 1902 exhibition honoring the composer.

▶ *€9.50 includes special exhibits, Tue-Sun 10:00-18:00, closed Mon, audioguide-€3, Friedrichstrasse 12, +43 1 587 5307, www.secession.at.*

The culmination of Klimt's *Beethoven Frieze:* A heavenly choir serenades two lovers.

The Naschmarkt is perfect for strolling, noshing, drinking, and people-watching.

▲Naschmarkt

In 1898, the city decided to cover up its Vienna River. The long, wide square they created was filled with a lively produce market that still bustles most days. Entering the "Belly of Vienna," note the two parallel lanes. The right lane consists of market stalls, while the left lane is mostly eateries. In recent years, many stalls have been taken over by hip bars and eateries, bringing a youthful vibe and fun new flavors to the market scene. Wander through spices, exotic fruits, olives, cheeses, baklava, and more. From here, the market progresses from cheaper sausage stands and Turkish *döner kebab* stalls to trendier (and more expensive) eateries and upscale stalls.

▶ *Mon-Fri 6:00-19:30, Sat until 18:00, closed Sun, closes earlier in winter; restaurants open until 23:00; ride the U-Bahn to Kettenbrückengasse, then walk the length of the market.*

SIGHTS BEYOND THE RING

▲▲Belvedere Palace (Schloss Belvedere)

This is the elegant palace of Prince Eugene of Savoy (1663-1736), the still much-appreciated conqueror of the Ottomans. Eugene, a Frenchman considered too short and too ugly to be in the service of Louis XIV, offered his services to the Habsburgs. He became the greatest military genius of his age, the savior of Austria, and the toast of Viennese society.

Today you can tour Eugene's lavish palace, see sweeping views of the gardens and the Vienna skyline, and enjoy world-class art starring Gustav Klimt (including *The Kiss*), French Impressionism, and a grab bag of other 19th- and early-20th-century artists. The palace complex includes the Upper Palace (art collection), smaller Lower Palace (historical rooms and temporary exhibits), the Belvedere 21 (contemporary art), and pleasantly beautiful Baroque-style gardens.

For our purposes, the Upper Palace is what matters. The palace's eclectic collection is tailor-made for browsing, but be aware that exhibits change frequently, so some of the things I mention here may not be on display. From the entrance, climb the staircase to the first floor and enter a grand red-and-gold, chandeliered **Marble Hall.** The ceiling fresco shows Eugene (in the center, wearing blue and pink) about to be crowned with a laurel wreath for his military victories and contributions to Vienna. *Belvedere* means "beautiful view," and the view from the Marble Hall is the most iconic of the city. Left to right, find the green dome of St. Peter's Church, the spire of St. Stephen's (where Eugene is buried, see the St. Stephen's Cathedral Tour chapter), and much nearer, the black dome of the Silesian Church. St. Stephen's

Belvedere Palace: Gardens, views, and…

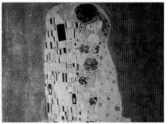

…fine art, starring Klimt's *The Kiss*

Jugendstil and the Vienna Secession

As Europe approached the dawn of a new (*nouveau*) century, artists began creating a truly new and free art style that left behind the stodginess of the 19th century. Though the Art Nouveau movement began in Paris and Belgium, each country gave it its own spin. In German-speaking lands, Art Nouveau was called Jugendstil (meaning "youth style").

Art Nouveau was forward-looking and modern, embracing the new technology of iron and glass. But it was also a reaction against the sheer ugliness of the mass-produced, boxy, rigidly geometrical art of the Industrial Age. Art Nouveau artists embraced nature and the sinuous curves of organic plant forms. Street lamps twist and bend like flower stems. Ironwork fountains sprout buds that squirt water. Art Nouveau was a total "look" that could be applied to furniture, jewelry, paintings, and even entire buildings.

Vienna's Art Nouveau/ Jugendstil movement is called "the Secession." Gustav Klimt, Otto Wagner, Egon Schiele, Oskar Kokoschka, and company looked to escape, or "secede," from conventionalism. The Secessionist motto was: "To each age its art, and to art its liberty."

spire is 400 feet tall, and no other tall buildings are allowed inside the Ringstrasse. The hills beyond—covered with vineyards—are where the Viennese love to go to sample new wine at *Heurigen* (wine gardens—see the Eating chapter).

Now head to the **East Wing.** Sumptuous paintings by **Gustav Klimt** and his contemporaries (including Monet) fill the rooms. You can get caught up in his fascination with the beauty and danger he saw in women. To Klimt, all art was erotic art. Even fully clothed, his women have a bewitching eroticism in a world full of pollen and pistils.

The famous painting *Judith* (1901) shows no biblical heroine—Klimt paints her as a high-society Viennese woman with an ostentatious dog-collar necklace. With half-closed eyes and slightly parted lips, she's dismissive...yet mysterious and bewitching. Holding the head of her biblical victim, she's the modern femme fatale.

At the far end is perhaps Klimt's best-known painting, *The Kiss,* where two lovers are wrapped up in the colorful gold-and-jeweled cloak of bliss. Klimt's woman is no longer dominating, but submissive, abandoning herself to her man in a fertile field and a vast universe.

While Klimt's works are seductive and otherworldly, **Egon Schiele**'s tend to be darker and more introspective. One of Schiele's most recognizable works, *The Embrace,* shows a couple engaged in an erotically charged, rippling moment of passion. *The Family,* a melancholy painting from 1918, is Schiele's last major painting—he and his pregnant wife died in the influenza epidemic that swept through Europe after World War I.

The rest of the Belvedere's collection goes through the whole range of 19th- and 20th-century art: Historicism, Romanticism, Impressionism, Realism, tired tourism, Expressionism, Art Nouveau, and early Modernism. The second floor up shows off early-19th-century paintings in the Biedermeier style. The final rooms display Renoir's ladies and Van Gogh's rough brushstrokes, from a time concerned with light and native landscapes.

On the opposite end of the delightfully manicured gardens (and covered by a separate ticket) is the Lower Palace where Prince Eugene actually hung his helmet. It also houses some generally good special exhibits, as well as the entrance to the privy garden and stables.

▶ *€18 for Upper Belvedere Palace only, €26 for Upper and Lower Palaces (and special exhibits), gardens-free; daily 10:00-18:00, grounds open until dusk; audioguide-€5; entrance at Prinz-Eugen-Strasse 27, +43 1 795 570, www.belvedere.at.*

The palace is a 20-minute walk south of the Ring. To get there from the center, catch tram #D at the opera house (direction: Absberggasse). Get off at the Schloss Belvedere stop (just below the Upper Palace gate), cross the street, walk uphill one block, go through the gate (on left), and look immediately to the right for the small building with the ticket office.

▲**Museum of Military History (Heeresgeschichtliches Museum)**
While much of the Habsburg Empire was built on strategic marriages rather than the spoils of war, a big part of Habsburg history is military. And this huge place, built about 1860 as an arsenal by Franz Josef, tells the story well with a thoughtful motto: "Wars belong in museums."

The museum's two floors hold a rich collection of artifacts and historic treasures from the times of Maria Theresa to Prince Eugene to Franz Josef. The particularly interesting 20th-century section on the ground floor includes exhibits devoted to Sarajevo in 1914 (with the car Franz Ferdinand rode in and the uniform he wore when he was assassinated), Chancellor Engelbert Dollfuss and the pre-Hitler Austrian Fascist party, the Anschluss, and World War II.

▶ *€7, includes good audioguide, free first Sun of the month; daily 9:00-17:00, +43 1 795 6110, www.hgm.at. It's a five-minute walk from the Quartier Belvedere tram/S-Bahn stop behind the Belvedere Palace.*

▲Kunst Haus Wien and Museum Hundertwasserhaus

This museum and nearby apartment complex are a hit with lovers of modern art, mixing the work and philosophy of local painter/environmentalist Friedensreich Hundertwasser (1928-2000), a.k.a. "100H2O."

Of the two sights here designed by Hundertwasser—the museum and the *haus* itself—the museum is best. Admire the museum's jaunty checkerboard exterior and lush greenery. Inside, you'll learn about the man's life and art; the walls are peppered with his fun philosophical quotes.

A 5- to 10-minute walk takes you to the Hundertwasserhaus (at Löwengasse and Kegelgasse). This complex of 50 apartments, subsidized by the government to provide affordable housing, was built in the 1980s as a breath of architectural fresh air in a city of boring, blocky apartment complexes. While not open to visitors, it's worth seeing for its fun and colorful patchwork exterior and the Hundertwasser festival of shops nearby. Don't miss the view from both streets to see the "tree tenants" and the internal winter garden that residents enjoy.

▶ *€11 for museum, €12 combo-ticket includes special exhibitions, open daily 10:00-18:00, audioguide-€3, +43 1 712 0491, www.kunsthauswien.com.*

It's located at Untere Weissgerberstrasse 13, near the Radetzkyplatz stop on trams #O and #1 (signs point the way). Take the U-Bahn to Landstrasse and either walk 10 minutes downhill (north) along Untere Viaduktgasse (a block east of the station), or transfer to tram #O (direction: Praterstern) and ride three stops to Radetzkyplatz.

▲Vienna Furniture Museum (Möbelmuseum)

Bizarre, sensuous, eccentric, or precious, this underappreciated collection (on four fascinating floors) is your peek at the Habsburgs'

The Hundertwasserhaus complex shows this unique designer's love of color and curvy lines.

furniture—from the empress' wheelchair ("to increase her fertility she was put on a rich diet and became corpulent") to the emperor's spittoon—all thoughtfully described in English. Evocative paintings help bring the furniture to life.

To avoid lines at the Schönbrunn Palace and the Hofburg Imperial Apartments, buy your Sisi Ticket here first or purchase in advance online (www.schoenbrunn.at).

▸ *€11.50, includes audioguide, covered by Sisi Ticket, Tue-Sun 10:00-17:00, closed Mon, Mariahilfer Strasse 88, main entrance around the corner at Andreasgasse 7, U: Zieglergasse, +43 1 5243 3570, www.moebelmuseumwien.at.*

▲Third Man Museum (Dritte Mann Museum)

Released in 1949 and voted one of the greatest films of all time by the British Film Institute, *The Third Man* is a Cold War thriller about a divided Vienna afraid of falling under Soviet rule. The museum has a vast collection of artifacts about the film, its popularity around the world, and postwar Vienna. *Third Man* fans will love the quirky movie artifacts, but even if you're just interested in Vienna in the pre- and postwar years, the museum is worthwhile.

▸ *€10, RS%—€2 discount with this book, Sat only 14:00-18:00, also guided tours at other times by appointment, tour lasts 80 minutes; U: Kettenbrückengasse, a long block south of the Naschmarkt at Pressgasse 25, +43 676 47 57 818, www.3mpc.net.*

ON VIENNA'S OUTSKIRTS

▲▲▲Schönbrunn Palace (Schloss Schönbrunn)

The Habsburgs' former summer residence, just a 10-minute subway ride from downtown Vienna, is second only to Versailles among Europe's grand palaces. The highlight of the vast complex's many sights is a tour of the Imperial Apartments where the Habsburg nobles lived (including Maria Theresa and her 16 children, and Franz Josef and Sisi).

📖 See the Schönbrunn Palace Tour chapter.

▲Prater Park (Wiener Prater)

Since the 1780s, this place has been Vienna's playground. For the tourist, the "Prater" is the sugary-smelling, tired, and sprawling

Horse-drawn carriages line up in front of Schönbrunn Palace.

amusement park (*Wurstelprater*). For locals, the "Prater" is the vast, adjacent green park with its three-mile-long, tree-lined main boulevard (Hauptallee). The park still tempts visitors with its huge 220-foot-tall, famous, and lazy Ferris wheel (*Riesenrad*), fun roller coasters, bumper cars, Lilliputian railroad, and endless eateries. Especially if you're traveling with kids, this is a fun place to share the evening with thousands of Viennese and tourists.

▶ *Park is free and always open; amusement park—rides cost €2-8 and run May-Oct roughly 10:00-22:00, but often later in good weather in summer, fewer rides open in off-season; U: Praterstern, www.prater. at. For a local-style family dinner, eat at* **Schweizerhaus** *(good food, great Czech Budvar—the original "Budweiser"—beer, classic conviviality) at the back of the park near the green tower.*

A Walk in the Vienna Woods (Wienerwald)
For a quick side-trip into the woods and out of the city, catch the U-4 subway line to Heiligenstadt, then bus #38A to Kahlenberg, where you'll enjoy great views and a café overlooking the city. From there, it's a peaceful 45-minute downhill hike to the *Heurigen* of Nussdorf to enjoy some new wine (see the Eating chapter).

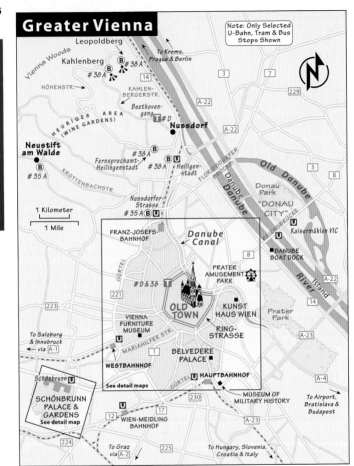

Greater Vienna

Note: Only Selected
U-Bahn, Tram & Bus
Stops Shown

Leopoldberg

To Krems,
Prague & Berlin

Vienna Woods

Kahlenberg

#38 A

#38 A

HÖHENSTR.

KAHLEN-
BERGERSTR.

A-22

Beethoven-
gang

#D

Nussdorf

A-22

HEURIGER AREA
(WINE GARDENS)

Neustift
am Walde

#38 A

Fernsprechamt-
Heilingenstadt

#38 A

Heiligen-
stadt

#35 A

KROTTENBACHSTR.

Nussdorfer-
Strasse

#35 A

FLORIDSDORFER BRÜCKE

Danube

Old Danube

Donau
Park

"DONAU
CITY"

3

8

REICHSBRÜCKE

Kaisermühlen VIC

FRANZ-
JOSEFS-
BAHNHOF

Danube
Canal

DANUBE
BOAT DOCK

8

PRATER
AMUSEMENT
PARK

GÜRTEL

#D & 38

221

223

OLD
TOWN

KUNST
HAUS WIEN

Prater
Park

A-22

Island River

14

VIENNA
FURNITURE
MUSEUM

RING-
STRASSE

A-23

To Salzburg
& Innsbruck
via A-1

MARIAHILFER STR.

1

BELVEDERE
PALACE

WESTBAHNHOF

GÜRTEL

HAUPTBAHNHOF

See detail maps

A-4

Schönbrunn

SCHÖNBRUNN
PALACE &
GARDENS
See detail map

17

230

MUSEUM OF
MILITARY HISTORY

To Airport,
Bratislava &
Budapest

12

WIEN-MEIDLING
BAHNHOF

A-23

224

To Graz
via A-2

225

To Hungary, Slovenia,
Croatia & Italy

1 Kilometer

1 Mile

14

3

7

229

3

8

Young Mozart came of age in Vienna.

The opera has cheap standing-room tix.

MUSIC SIGHTS

For music lovers, Vienna is an opportunity to make pilgrimages to the homes (now mostly small museums) of favorite composers. If you're a fan of Schubert, Brahms, Haydn, Beethoven, or Mozart, there's a sight for you. But I find these homes inconveniently located and generally underwhelming. Instead, I prefer to tour the opera house (or get standing-room tickets for a performance), take in a concert, attend a musical Sunday Mass at the Augustinian Church, visit the Haus der Musik, or browse the Collection of Historic Musical Instruments at the World Museum Vienna.

DAY TRIPS (AND BEYOND)

Melk and the Danube Valley (rustic pastoral beauty) are an hour-plus by train. Bratislava (the up-and-coming capital of Slovakia) is an hour by train (or a longer boat ride that's not as scenic as it sounds).

Still farther, Vienna is a good jumping-off point by train for musical Salzburg (3 hours), charming Hallstatt (4 hours), Innsbruck (4.5 hours), Mauthausen Concentration Camp Memorial (2 hours), Budapest, Hungary (2.5 hours), and Prague, Czech Republic (4 hours).

Activities

You'll never run out of things to do in Vienna. This chapter offers suggestions for tours, shopping, and entertainment.

Besides taking in a concert in the birthplace of what we call classical music, you can spend an evening enjoying art, watching a classic film, or sipping Viennese wine in a village wine garden. Save some energy for Vienna after dark.

If powdered wigs and opera singers in Viking helmets aren't your thing, Vienna has plenty of alternatives. Take a tour by bus, bike, or horse-and-buggy. Or window-shop your way through the old town. The activities in this chapter allow you to take it easy and enjoy the Viennese good life.

TOURS

🎧 To sightsee on your own, download my free **Vienna City Walk, St. Stephen's Cathedral,** and **Ringstrasse** audio tours (see sidebar on page 11 for details).

Bus Tours

Two companies (**Big Bus**—red, **Vienna Sightseeing**—yellow) offer a complicated and busy program of hop-on, hop-off bus tours. While the ride can be scenic, gets you from sight to sight conveniently, and offers a stress-free overview, the recorded narration is almost worthless. Both companies offer 24-, 48-, and 72-hour tickets, including a circular bus route (with departures every 20 minutes) and options to add river cruises and walking tours. Prices start at around €32 for 24 hours. If you're adept at public transit, a good walker, and can read this guidebook, these hop-on, hop-off tours are not a good value.

Horse-and-Buggy Tour

These traditional 19th-century horse-and-buggies, called *Fiaker,* take rich romantics on clip-clop tours lasting 20 minutes (Old Town—€55),

40 minutes (Old Town and the Ring–€95), or one hour (all the above, but more thorough–€120). You can share the ride and cost with up to four people (some may allow five). Because it's a kind of guided tour, talk to a few drivers before choosing a carriage, and pick someone who's fun and speaks English.

Bike Tour

Pedal Power's tours cover the central district in three hours and go daily at 10:00 from May to September (€37/person, RS%—10 percent with this book, €20 extra to keep bike for the day, just beyond the Ring near the opera house at Bösendorferstrasse 5, +43 1 729 7234, www. pedalpower.at). They also rent bikes *sans* tour.

Walking Tours

The TI's ***Walks in Vienna*** brochure lists more than a dozen walks— many given in English, all for €20. Their basic 1.5-hour "Vienna at First Glance" introductory walk is usually offered daily throughout the summer (leaves from in front of the TI, reservations smart, +43 664 260 4388, www.wienguide.at).

Good Vienna Tours runs a "pay what you like" 2.5-hour,

Vienna's fascinating history makes the city ideal for touring with a local guide.

English-only walk through the city center. While my Vienna City Walk is much more succinct, this can be an entertaining ramble with a local telling stories of the city. Just show up (pay what you think it's worth at the end—no coins, paper only, daily departures at 10:00 and 14:00, also at 17:00 July-Aug, meet at fountain at tip of Albertina across from TI, mobile +43 664 554 4315, www.goodviennatours.eu).

Local Guides: Lisa Zeiler is a good storyteller with years of guiding experience (€160/2 hours, +43 699 1203 7550, lisa.zeiler@gmx.at); **Adrienn Bartek-Rhomberg** offers themed walks in the city as well as Schönbrunn Palace tours (€200/3 hours, €370/full day on foot, €360 "Panorama City Tour"—a 4-hour minibus and walking tour for up to six people, +43 650 826 6965, www.experience-vienna.at, office@experience-vienna.at); **Wolfgang Höfler** has a knack for having psychoanalytical fun with history, and he'll take you around on foot or by bike (€180/2 hours, €50 for each additional hour, bike tours-€180/3 hours, +43 676 304 4940, www.vienna-aktivtours.com, hofwolf@gmail.com); **Gerhard Strassgschwandtner** is passionate about history in all its marvelous complexity (€160/2 hours, +43 676 475 7818, www.special-vienna.com, gerhard@special-vienna.com).

SHOPPING

Vienna—a city that loves beautiful things—brings out the shopper in almost everyone. You won't need a guidebook to find plenty of shops selling Sisi fridge magnets, Klimt jewel-cases, Beethoven music boxes, and the ubiquitous chocolate Mozart Balls. Here are a few other ideas to consider.

Traditional Austrian Clothing

If you're interested in picking up a classy felt suit or dirndl, you'll find shops all over town. Most central is the fancy Loden-Plankl shop, with a vast world of traditional Austrian formalwear upstairs (across from the Hofburg, at Michaelerplatz 6). The Tostmann Trachten shop is the ultimate for serious shopping. Frau Tostmann's place is like a shrine to traditional Austrian and folk clothing (called *Tracht*)—handmade and very expensive (Schottengasse 3A, three-minute walk from Am Hof, +43 1 533 5331).

Pop into J & L Lobmeyr for an elegant Viennese shopping experience.

Take home a Sisi souvenir...   ...or traditional dirndl or lederhosen.

Artsy Gifts

Vienna's museum shops are some of Europe's best. The design store in the Museum of Applied Arts (MAK) is a delight; the shops of the Albertina Museum, Kunsthistorisches Museum, Belvedere Palace, Kunst Haus Wien, and the MuseumsQuartier museums are also particularly good. For the best in Austrian design and handicrafts, visit Österreichische Werkstätten, a shop/gallery just south of the cathedral (Mon-Sat 10:00-18:00, closed Sun, Kärntner Strasse 6, www.oew.at).

Window Shopping

The narrow streets north and west of the cathedral are sprinkled with old-fashioned shops that seem to belong to another era, carrying a curiously narrow range of items for sale (old clocks, men's ties, gloves, and so on). South of the cathedral, dedicated window shoppers will enjoy the Dorotheum auction house and the free glass museum at J & L Lobmeyr Crystal.

VAT and Customs

Getting a VAT Refund: If you purchase more than €75.01 worth of goods at a single store, you may be eligible to get a refund of the 20 percent Value-Added Tax (VAT). Get more details from your merchant or see www.ricksteves.com/vat.

   Customs for American Shoppers: You can take home $800 worth of items per person duty-free, once every 31 days. You can bring in one liter of alcohol duty-free. For details on allowable goods, customs rules, and duty rates, visit http://help.cbp.gov.

ENTERTAINMENT AND NIGHTLIFE

Take in a concert, opera, or other musical event. Enjoy a leisurely dinner (and people-watching) in the stately old town or the atmospheric Spittelberg quarter. Visit a museum that stays open late. Or sip wine with the locals in a wine garden.

For a current list of cultural events, pick up the TI's free quarterly brochure, *Spot,* or download it at Wien.info.

Classical Music

Vienna still thrives as Europe's music capital. On any given evening, you'll have your choice of opera, Strauss waltzes, Mozart chamber concerts, and lighthearted musicals.

In Vienna, it's music *con brio* from September through June, reaching a symphonic climax during the Vienna Festival each May and June. In July and August, the serious music companies are—like you—on vacation. But even then, music lovers have options.

The major orchestral venues are the Wiener Musikverein (home of the Vienna Philharmonic Orchestra) and the Wiener Konzerthaus (various events). Most tickets run from €45 to €60 (plus a stiff booking fee when purchased in advance by phone or online, or through a box office like the one at the TI). A few venues charge as little as €30. While it's easy to book tickets online long in advance, spontaneity is also workable, as there are invariably people selling their extra tickets at face value or less outside the door before concert time. If you call a concert hall directly, they can advise you on the availability of (cheaper) tickets at the door. Cheap standing-room tickets to top-notch music and opera are generally available an hour before each performance.

Vienna Boys' Choir (Wiener Sängerknaben)

The boys sing (from a high balcony, heard but not seen) at the 9:15 Sunday Mass from mid-September through June in the Hofburg's **Imperial Music Chapel** (Hofmusikkapelle). Reserved seats must be booked in advance (€12-43; reserve online or email office@hofmusikkapelle.gv.at; call +43 1 533 9927 for information only—they can't book tickets at this number; www.hofmusikkapelle.gv.at).

Standing room inside is free for the first 60 who line up, or you can simply swing by and stand in the narthex just outside, where you can hear the boys and see the Mass on a TV monitor. The boys

also perform at the **MuTh** concert hall on some Fridays at 17:00 during peak season (€39-62, Am Augartenspitz 1 in Augarten park, U: Taborstrasse, +43 1 347 8080, www.muth.at, tickets@muth.at).

Vienna State Opera (Wiener Staatsoper)

The state opera company puts on 300 performances a year (Sept-June). Even though the expensive seats normally sell out long in advance, the opera is subsidized by the state, so affordable seats are often available. Main-floor seats go for €79-240; bargain hunters get limited-view seats for €16-30. You can book tickets online (www.wiener-staatsoper.at) or in person at the opera's box office on Kärntner Strasse (Mon-Sat 10:00-18:00 or until one hour before each performance, Sun until 13:00).

Unless a top tenor is in town, it's easy to get one of 460 standing-room tickets (*Stehplätze,* €15 up top or €18 downstairs, one ticket/person). A side door (middle of building, on the Operngasse side) opens 90 minutes before curtain time. Just walk straight in, then head right until you see the ticket booth marked Stehplätze. Spaces are numbered—show up early and try for the "Parterre" section, where you'll end up dead-center at stage level, directly under the Emperor's Box.

Three hours is a lot of opera. I'd buy a standing-room ticket and plan to just watch the first part of the show. Before cutting out, have a glass of champagne at the opera's most glamorous bar (on the first floor, center front).

Each spring and fall the opera projects several performances live on a huge screen on its building, puts out chairs for the public to enjoy...and it's all free. Schedules for these Oper Live am Platz are posted all around the opera building and listed in the *Spot* brochure and at www.wiener-staatsoper.at.

Costumed salesmen push touristy concerts.

In Vienna, music is everywhere.

Touristy Mozart and Strauss Concerts

A number of venues offer chamber music, played by musicians in historic costumes, in traditional settings. Pesky wigged-and-powdered Mozarts peddle tickets in the streets. The musicians are usually quite good, the performances are casual, and while lots of tour groups attend, tourists generally enjoy the evening. To sort through your options, check with the ticket office in the TI. Savvy locals suggest getting the cheapest tickets, as no one seems to care if cheapskates move up to fill unsold pricier seats.

Of the many fine venues in Vienna, I have two reliable favorites: The Sala Terrena at Mozarthaus (don't confuse it with the Mozarthaus Vienna Museum on Domgasse) offers intimate concerts in a small room decorated in Venetian Renaissance style (€42-69, Wed, Fri, and Sun at 19:30, Sat at 18:00; near St. Stephen's Cathedral at Singerstrasse 7, +43 1 911 9077, www.mozarthaus.at). The Kursalon—the hall where Johann "Waltz King" Strauss himself directed wildly popular concerts 100 years ago—now hosts two-hour shows mixing ballet, waltzes, and a 15-piece orchestra (€63-105, concerts generally nightly at 20:30, Johannesgasse 33 at corner of Parkring, tram #2: Weihburggasse or U: Stadtpark, +43 1 512 5790 to check on availability—generally no problem to reserve—or buy online at www.soundofvienna.at).

Other Musical Options

For less-serious operettas and musicals, try the Vienna Volksoper, located along the Gürtel, west of the city center (see *Spot* brochure or ask at TI for schedule, Währinger Strasse 78, +43 1 5144 43670, www.volksoper.at). The intimate Theater an der Wien (from 1801) treats Vienna's music lovers to a different opera every month (except

The Kursalon combines music and dance.

Hear Mozart hits in atmospheric settings.

Sightseeing After Dark

Every night in Vienna some sights stay open late. My Vienna City Walk and Ring-strasse Tram Tour both work well at night, amid floodlit monuments:

St. Stephen's Cathedral: Nightly until 22:00 (but main nave closes earlier). See page 35.

Haus der Musik: Nightly until 22:00. See page 132.

Albertina Museum: Wed and Fri until 21:00. See page 129.

Natural History Museum: Wed until 21:00. See page 134.

Kunsthistorisches Museum: Thu until 21:00. See page 97.

World Museum Vienna: Tue until 21:00. See page 127.

summer)—with a contemporary setting and modern interpretation (facing the Naschmarkt at Linke Wienzeile 6, +43 1 58 885, www.theater-wien.at).

Modern Broadway-style musicals (in German with English subtitles) play at several venues (€50-110). Same-day tickets are sometimes available at a discount directly from the theater (from 14:00 until 18:00); the Wien Ticket pavilion next to the opera house also sells tickets (daily 10:00-19:00). You can also reserve (full-price) tickets by phone or online (+43 1 58 885, line answered daily 8:00-20:00, www.wien-ticket.at).

After-Hours Neighborhoods

Vienna is a great place to just be out and about on a balmy evening amid bars, cafés, trendy restaurants, and theaters. The obvious choice is the historic center around St. Stephen's Cathedral and the Graben. Donaukanal (the Danube Canal) is especially popular in the summer for its imported beaches. At Naschmarkt, after the produce stalls close up, the bars and eateries bring new life to the place. The

Evenings are pleasant at Prater Park...

...or at a café dining al fresco.

MuseumsQuartier is surrounded by far-out museums and a youthful scene of bars with local students filling the courtyard. The **Prater** amusement park attracts families and fun (see the Sights chapter), while the **wine gardens** (*Heurigen*) north of downtown are a fun getaway (see the Eating chapter).

A convivial, free-to-everyone people scene erupts each evening in summer (July-Aug) on **Rathausplatz,** the welcoming park in front of City Hall (right on the Ringstrasse). Thousands of people keep a food circus of simple stalls busy. When darkness falls, everyone takes a seat to enjoy a movie—mostly films of opera and classical concerts, but with some jazz and R&B, too (www.filmfestival-rathausplatz.at, programs generally last about 2 hours, starts at dark—between 21:30 in July and 20:30 in Aug).

English Cinema

Several great theaters offer three or four screens of English movies nightly (€8-11). **English Cinema Haydn** is near my recommended hotels on Mariahilfer Strasse (Mariahilfer Strasse 57, +43 1 587 2262, www.haydnkino.at), and **Artis International Cinema** is right in the town center a few minutes from the cathedral (Schultergasse 5, +43 1 535 6570, www.cineplexx.at/center/artis-international). **Burg Kino,** a block from the opera house, offers modern and classic films in English and often shows *The Third Man,* set in postwar Vienna's shadowy Cold War world (usually two or three showings weekly, check schedule at www.burgkino.at; Opernring 19, +43 1 587 8406).

Film fans can watch *The Third Man* at Burg Kino or visit the Third Man Museum (pictured).

Sleeping

Accommodations in Vienna are plentiful and relatively cheap compared to other European cities. I've grouped my hotel listings into two—well, really three—neighborhoods: The old town (within the Ring) is most central, atmospheric, and pricey. Mariahilfer Strasse (stretching from the Ring to the Westbahnhof) is less classy but a better value, and has two distinct areas: Its east end is more gentrified, while the west end (near the train station) is rougher.

I like hotels that are clean, central, reasonably priced, friendly, small enough to have a hands-on owner and stable staff, and run with a respect for Austrian traditions. Double rooms listed in this book average around €100 (including a private bathroom). They range from a low of roughly €60 (very simple, with toilet and shower down the hall) to €300 (maximum plumbing and more).

Vienna Hotels

Expect to pay more for rooms within the Ring. For less expensive accommodations, look at my recommendations around Mariahilfer Strasse. Expect rates to spike for conventions and to drop in low season (usually Nov and Jan-March). For some travelers, short-term, Airbnb-type rentals can be a good alternative; search for places in my recommended hotel neighborhoods.

Many of the hotels I've listed here share buildings with other businesses or residences, which can mean lots of stairs or (hopefully) an elevator. Viennese elevators and stairwells can be confusing: In most of Europe, 0 is the ground floor, and 1 is the first floor up (our "second floor"). But in Vienna, thanks to a Habsburg-legacy quirk, older buildings have at least one extra "mezzanine" floor (labeled on elevators as P, H, M, and/or A) between the ground floor and the "first" floor, so floor 1 can actually be what we'd call the second, third, or even fourth floor.

Making Reservations

Reserve your rooms as soon as you've pinned down your travel dates. Book your room directly via email or phone, or through the hotel's official website (not a booking website).

The hotelier wants to know:
- Type(s) of room(s) you want and number of guests
- Number of nights you'll stay
- Arrival and departure dates, written European-style as day/month (18/06 or 18 June)
- Special requests (en suite bathroom, cheapest room, twin beds vs. double bed, quiet room)
- Applicable discounts (such as a Rick Steves discount, cash discount, or promotional rate)

Most places will request a credit-card number to hold your room. If the hotel's website doesn't have a secure form where you can enter the number directly, share this info via a phone call. If you must cancel, it's courteous—and smart—to do so with as much notice as possible. Cancellation policies can be strict; read the fine print.

Always call or email to reconfirm your reservation a few days in advance. For B&Bs or very small hotels, I call again on my arrival day to tell my host what time to expect me (especially if arriving after 17:00).

Sleep Code

Dollar signs reflect average rates for a standard double room with breakfast in high season.

$$$$	**Splurge:** Most rooms €200
$$$	**Pricier:** €150–200
$$	**Moderate:** €90–150
$	**Budget:** €50–90
¢	**Backpacker:** Under €50
RS%	**Rick Steves discount**

Unless otherwise noted, credit cards are accepted, hotel staff speak basic English, and free Wi-Fi is available. If the listing includes **RS%**, request a Rick Steves discount.

SLEEPING

Budget Tips

Comparison-shop by checking prices at several hotels (on each hotel's own website, on a booking site, or by email). For the best deal, book directly with the hotel. Ask for a discount if paying in cash.

A short-term rental in an apartment is a popular alternative, especially if you plan to settle in for several nights. You can usually find a rental that's comparable to—and cheaper than—a hotel room with similar amenities. Plus, you'll get a behind-the-scenes peek into how locals live. Websites such as Airbnb, Flipkey, Booking.com, and VRBO let you browse a wide range of properties.

A hostel (*Jugendherberge*) provides cheap beds where you sleep alongside strangers for about €25 per night. Travelers of any age are welcome if they don't mind dorm-style accommodations and meeting other travelers. Most hostels offer kitchen facilities, guest computers, Wi-Fi, and a self-service laundry. Hostels almost always provide bedding, but the towel's up to you (though you can usually rent one). Family and private rooms are often available.

OLD TOWN

Within the Ringstrasse, walking distance to sights, pricier but more atmospheric—the classiest Vienna experience. U: Stephansplatz or Karlsplatz

$$$$ Hotel am Stephansplatz Four-star business hotel, plush but not over-the-top, superb breakfast, air-con, elevator.

Stephansplatz 9, +43 1 534 050, https://hotelamstephansplatz.at

$$$$ Pension Nossek On pedestrian-only Graben, modern and well-appointed rooms, air-con, elevator.

Graben 17, +43 1 5337 0410, www.pension-nossek.at

$$$ Aviano Boutique Hotel Friendly, family-run, great value, 17 rooms with Baroque frills, breakfast extra, fans, coolest rooms face courtyard, elevator.

Marco d'Avianogasse 1, +43 1 512 8330, www.avianoboutiquehotel.com

$$$ Hotel Pertschy Big and elegantly creaky, huge rooms with Baroque touches, ask for quiet room, fans, elevator.

Habsburgergasse 5, +43 1 534 490, www.pertschy.com

$$$ Hotel zur Wiener Staatsoper Quiet with traditional elegance, large rooms with chandeliers and fancy carpets, air-con, elevator.

Krugerstrasse 11, +43 1 513 1274, www.hotel-staatsoper.at

$$$ Pension A und A Nine rooms with contemporary style, white minimalist hallways, air-con.

Habsburgergasse 3, +43 1 890 5128, www.aundapension.com

$$$ Hotel Das Tigra 17th-century building where Mozart reportedly stayed, classic rooms with modern touches, air-con.

Tiefer Graben 14, +43 1 533 96410, www.hotel-tigra.at

$$ Motel One Staatsoper Around 400 smallish, modern rooms, nicer option for budget travelers, no triples but can slip in a child under 6 for free, breakfast extra, air-con, elevator.

Elisabethstrasse 5, +43 1 585 0505, www.motel-one.com

$$ Pension Suzanne Baroque and doily, run with class, packed with Viennese antiques, apartment available for up to 6, fans, elevator.

Walfischgasse 4, +43 1 513 2507, www.pension-suzanne.at

$$ Pension Neuer Markt Perfectly central, comfy but faded pink rooms, cruise-ship ambience, in hot weather request a courtyard-side room when you reserve, fans, tiny elevator.

Seilergasse 9, +43 1 512 2316, www.hotelpension.at

MARIAHILFER STRASSE—EAST

Lively street on convenient U-3 line between Westbahnhof and downtown; inexpensive stores and cafés; east end of the street is closer to downtown and a short walk to the Museum District/Spittelberg and the Naschmarkt. U: Zieglergasse or Neubaugasse.

$$$ Hotel Kugel Run with style by Johannes and Christina Roller, 25 unique rooms, most with canopy beds, junior suites offer modern alternative, wonderful breakfast, fans.

Siebensterngasse 43, +43 1 523 3355, www.hotelkugel.at

$$$ Hotel Gilbert Near MuseumsQuartier, a modern break from old Vienna, cozy bohemian-inspired lounge spaces attract a young clientele, air-con.

Breite Gasse 9, +43 1 523 1345, www.hotel-gilbert.at

$$ NH Collection Wien Zentrum Stylish-but-passionless business hotel, 73 rooms, a few "suites" for families, breakfast extra, air-con, elevator.

Mariahilfer Strasse 78, +43 1 524 5600, www.nh-hotels.com

$$ Hotel Pension Corvinus Run by a hardworking Hungarian family, 15 bright and spacious rooms, cash discount, family rooms and apartments, espresso machines, air-con, elevator.

Mariahilfer Strasse 57, +43 1 587 7239, www.corvinus.at

$ K&T Boardinghouse Five modern and spacious rooms, first floor of quiet building, cash only but reserve with credit card or PayPal, 2-night minimum, no breakfast, pay air-con.

Chwallagasse 2, +43 676 553 6063, www.ktboardinghouse.at

MARIAHILFER STRASSE—WEST

Near the Westbahnhof, these hotels (and several hostels) offer the same convenient U-Bahn connection to downtown, but they're generally less atmospheric and in a rougher neighborhood. U: Westbahnhof.

$$ Motel One Westbahnhof Rooms with modern flair, vibrant lobby with spaces to unwind, no triples but you can slip in a child under 6 for free, breakfast extra, air-con.

Europaplatz 3, +43 1 359 350, www.motel-one.com

$$ Hotel Ibis Wien Mariahilf Impersonal high-rise hotel with American charm, bright and comfortable cookie-cutter rooms, breakfast extra, air-con, elevator.

Mariahilfer Gürtel 22, +43 1 59 998, www.accorhotels.com

¢ Hostel Ruthensteiner Small and cozy, 100 beds in 4-to-8-bed dorms, private rooms available, breakfast extra, laundry, bike rental.

Robert-Hamerling-Gasse 24, +43 1 893 4202, www.hostelruthensteiner.com

¢ Westend City Hostel One block from Westbahnhof and Mariahilfer Strasse, well-run, quiet after 20:00, 180 beds in 4-to-12-bed dorms each with own bath, cash only, private rooms available, elevator, laundry.

Fügergasse 3, +43 1 597 6729, www.viennahostel.at

¢ Wombat's City Hostel 250 beds and generous public spaces, bar, 4-6 beds/room, private rooms available, near Naschmarkt.

Rechte Wienzeile 35, +43 1 897 2336, www.wombats-hostels.com

¢ Hostel Wien Classic, well-run, official youth hostel, 260 beds, private rooms available, always open, no curfew, coin-op laundry.

Myrthengasse 7, +43 1 523 6316, www.1070vienna.at

MORE HOTELS IN VIENNA
If my top listings are full, here are some others to consider.

$$$$ Hotel Domizil Near Stephansplatz, 43 bright rooms, neat as a pin.

Schulerstrasse 14, +43 1 513 3199, www.hoteldomizil.at

$$$$ Hotel Astoria Just off Kärntner Strasse, Old World hotel, 128 classy rooms, entrance at Führichgasse 1.

Kärntner Strasse 32, +43 1 515 77, www.austria-trend.at/hotel-astoria

$$$ Theaterhotel & Suites Near City Hall, shiny gem on fun shopping street.

Josefstädter Strasse 22, +43 1 405 3648, www.theaterhotel-wien.at

$$$ Hotel Marc Aurel Near Schwedenplatz, affordable, plain business-class hotel, modern rooms, air-con.

Marc Aurel Strasse 8, +43 1 533 3640, www.hotel-marcaurel.com

Eating

The Viennese appreciate the fine points of life, and right up there with good music is good eating.

The city has many atmospheric restaurants, serving top-notch cuisine with Hungarian and Bohemian flavors. In addition to restaurants, you'll find some uniquely Viennese institutions: the city's café culture and its *Heuriger* wine pubs.

My listings are (mostly) in three atmospheric neighborhoods: First is the **old town,** clustered near St. Stephen's, the opera house, and the atmospheric lanes of Am Hof Square. In the Museum District (just west of the Ring) are the cobbled lanes of **Spittelberg.** Along and near **Mariahilfer Strasse** (with many recommended hotels) you'll find reasonable cafés serving all types of cuisine.

No matter where you dine, expect it to be *gemütlich*—a much-prized Austrian virtue meaning an atmosphere of relaxed coziness.

When in Vienna

For breakfast, I eat at the hotel (bread, meat, cheese, pastries, yogurt, cereal) or grab a pastry and coffee at a café. Traditionally, the Austrian lunch (12:00-14:00) is a big meal (many restaurants offer dinner-size lunch specials), though health-conscious Viennese of today may choose lighter fare. In between meals, I might stop at a takeout stand for a wurst. In the late afternoon, the Viennese enjoy a beverage with friends at an outdoor table on a lively square. Dinner (18:00-21:00) might be the time to slow down and savor a multicourse restaurant meal.

Restaurant Etiquette

Full-service, sit-down restaurants in Austria operate much like restaurants everywhere, but there are a few small differences in etiquette.

Tipping is not necessary (because a service charge is included in the menu price), but a tip of about 5-10 percent is a nice reward for good service. Give the tip directly to your server. Austrians prefer not leaving coins on the table. So, for a €10 meal, they might tip €1 by paying with a €20 bill and telling the waiter the total they wish to pay: *"Elf, bitte"*—"Eleven, please"—to get €9 change.

Restaurants in touristed areas may add a "tip is not included" line, in English, to the bottom of the bill. This is misleading, as the prices on any menu in Austria *do* include service. I wouldn't tip one cent at a restaurant that includes this note.

Austrians pay for bottled water with their meal (*Mineralwasser mit/ ohne Gas*—with/without carbonation), and tap water (*Leitungswasser*) may cost around €0.50. You might be charged for bread you've eaten from the basket on the table; have the waiter take it away if you don't want it. Many restaurants are closed Sunday.

Many places offer pleasant outdoor seating in good weather; there's usually no extra charge to sit outside. Most restaurants offer a *"Menü"*—a fixed-price meal—at lunchtime on weekdays (typically around €10 for a main course plus soup or salad). The best dish on any menu is often the house specialty. For smaller portions, order from the *kleine Hunger* (small hunger) section of the menu.

Good service is relaxed service—only a rude waiter will rush you. When you want the bill, say, *"Rechnung* (REHKH-noong), *bitte."* To wish others "Happy eating!" offer a cheery *"Guten Appetit!"*

Restaurant Code

Dollar signs reflect the cost of a typical main course.

$$$$ **Splurge:** Most main courses over €20
$$$ **Pricier:** €15-20
$$ **Moderate:** €10-15
$ **Budget:** Under €10

A wurst stand or other takeout spot is **$**; a beer hall, *Biergarten,* or basic sit-down eatery is **$$**; a casual but more upscale restaurant is **$$$**; and a swanky splurge is **$$$$**.

Beisls, Wurst, Cafés, and More

Besides fancy restaurants, there are other, less-formal places to fill the tank.

Other Restaurants: I love *Beisls.* A *Beisl* (BYE-zul) is a neighborhood pub that serves hearty food and drinks at an affordable price. Ask your hotel to recommend a good *Beisl.* Global cuisine is popular, especially Asian, Turkish (good values), and Italian. Hotels often serve fine food. A *Gaststätte* is just a simple, less-expensive restaurant.

Cheap Takeout Meals and Picnics: Vienna makes it easy to turn a picnic into a first-class affair. Grab something to go and enjoy a bench in a lively square or leafy park. It's easy to find sandwiches and boxed salads at bakeries, delis, and supermarkets; try *Wurstsemmel* (a sausage sandwich) or *Schnitzelsemmel* (a schnitzel sandwich). Other cheap eateries include department-store cafeterias and *Schnellimbiss* (fast-food) stands. *Döner kebab* kiosks serve shaved meat and vegetables wrapped in pita bread.

Best of the Wurst: In Austria, you're never far from a *Würstelstand* (sausage stand). The wurst, usually pork sausage, comes in many varieties. *Bratwurst* is a generic term that simply means "grilled sausage." A *Burenwurst* is what we'd call "kielbasa." There's also *Weisswurst, Liverwurst,* and so on. Generally, the darker the weenie, the spicier it is.

At sausage stands, wurst usually comes on a paper plate with your choice of bread (*Brot*) or roll (*Semmel*), and with ketchup or mustard—sweet (*süss*) or sharp (*scharf*).

Americans call their plain sausage a *Wiener* after the city of

Dine in a woodsy medieval interior...   ...or outside, usually at no extra charge.

Vienna—a "Wien"-er. But the guy who invented the weenie actually studied in Frankfurt. When he moved to Vienna, he named his creation for his old hometown...a Frankfurter. Only in Vienna are Wieners called Frankfurters. Got it?

Vienna's Café Culture: In Vienna, the living room is down the street at the neighborhood coffeehouse. These classic institutions—many with a tradition stretching back generations—offer newspapers, pastries, sofas, elegant ambience, and "take all the time you want" charm for the price of a cup of coffee. Most serve light lunches, and some might have a more ambitious menu, but the focus here is on drinks. Each classic café has its individual character (and characters). Adopt an unhurried attitude, ignore the sometimes-shabby patina, roll with the famously grumpy waiters, and immerse yourself in the coffee experience, Vienna style.

Vienna—arguably the European birthplace of coffee—serves many of the same drinks (espresso, cappuccino) served in American or Italian coffee shops. There's some uniquely Austrian coffee lingo: A *Mélange* is like a cappuccino, a *Verlängerter* ("lengthened") is an Americano, and a *Verkehrt* ("upside-down") is a short latte.

Traditional Austrian Cuisine

Traditional Austrian dishes tend to be meat-heavy and hearty (although fish is very popular and generally good in this landlocked country). Much "Austrian" cooking is actually the legacy of their former empire, which included Hungary and Bohemia.

Main Dishes: The classic Austrian dish—and a standby on menus—is Wiener schnitzel (a veal cutlet that's been pounded flat, breaded, and fried). Pork schnitzel, which is cheaper, is also common.

Austrian white wines go well with local cuisine.

For beer, try a lager or a lemony *Radler*.

Austrian *Gulasch,* a meat stew, is a favorite comfort food. Chicken and pork come in all varieties—try *Schweinsbraten* (pork with dumplings and sauerkraut). *Tafelspitz* is boiled beef served with vegetables. For a meal-sized salad, order a *Salatteller.*

Sides: Common side dishes include *Knödel* (dumplings), *Spätzle* (little noodles), *Eiernockerl* (egg noodles), potatoes, and salads. *Spargel* (asparagus, white or green) is a must in May and June. Soups are popular, especially *Speckknödel* (ham-filled dumplings served in broth) and *Frittatensuppe* (beef broth with thin strips of crêpe).

Drinks: Austria specializes in fine boutique wines that are generally not exported and therefore not well-known. The wine (65 percent white) from the Danube River Valley and eastern Austria is particularly good. Good-quality wines are often available by the glass—an Achtel (4 oz) or a Viertel (8 oz). If you order *"Ein Viertel Weisswein, bitte—trocken,"* you'll get a glass of white wine that's *"trocken"*—dry. *Halbtrocken* is medium, and *süss* is sweet. Austria's signature wine is the *Grüner Veltliner*—a dry white, drunk young, that pairs well with food. In summer, locals also enjoy a refreshing *gespritzer Wein*— wine with sparkling water. Because so many white wines are best young, Austrians enjoy drinking the new wine at wine gardens called *Heurigen* (see later).

For beer, Austrians prefer light brews—lager (*Märzen*) and *Pils.* Also common are *Weissbier* (yeasty and wheat-based), *Bock* (hoppy seasonal ale), and *Radler* (beer with lemon soda). Vienna's local brewery is Ottakringer. When you order beer on tap *(vom Fass),* you can ask for *ein Pfiff* (about 7 oz), *ein Seidel* (10 oz), *ein Krügerl* (17 oz), or *eine Mass* (a whole liter—about a quart).

Austrians enjoy a wide range of local, nonalcoholic spritz drinks

Take a break from sightseeing to enjoy Vienna's famous pastries.

such as *Apfelsaft gespritzt* (apple juice with sparkling water), *Spezi* (Coke and orange soda), and the über-Austrian *Almdudler* (similar to ginger ale).

Dessert: While you're sure to have *Apfelstrudel* (apple-pie filling wrapped in wafer-thin pastry), try *Topfenstrudel,* too (with sweet cheese and raisins). *Palatschinken* (sweet filled crêpes) have Hungarian origins. The very Austrian *Kaiserschmarrn* consists of fluffy, caramelized crêpe strips topped with fruit, raisins, and/or nuts. Everywhere you'll see Mozart Balls (*Mozartkugeln*)—a chocolate confection wrapped with the composer's likeness that's become practically a symbol of Austria. The Fürst brand is handmade and authentic (first made in 1890); other brands are Reber (high quality) and Mirabell (biggest seller). And then there's Vienna's famous chocolate cake—Sacher torte. It's best with a dollop of *Schlagobers* (whipped cream). *Guten Appetit!*

Wein in Wien: Vienna's Wine Gardens

Sipping wine on a balmy evening under a leafy canopy, surrounded by the very vineyards that produced it, is a typically Viennese experience. A *Heuriger* (HOY-rih-gehr)—the wine equivalent of a beer garden—lets you enjoy wines by the glass and food from a buffet, in a pleasant atmosphere, indoors or out. These wine gardens are named for their specialty: the new wine *(heurig)* that vintners break out every November 11 and serve for the following 365 days. Some *Heurigen* have live (traditional) music or play zones for kids.

The experience is best in good weather, but you can eat indoors, too. Most *Heurigen* open up in the afternoon (generally between 14:00 and 16:00) and close late (about 24:00), but some are closed in winter.

Before going anywhere, consider a pretty good *Heuriger* right in the city center: Gigerl Stadtheuriger (see page 177). But it's surprisingly easy—and rewarding—to leave the city for a slower-paced world away from the tourist crowds.

Getting There: I recommend the Nussdorf neighborhood on the northern outskirts of town (see the "Greater Vienna" map). To get here from downtown Vienna, take tram #D from the Ringstrasse (get on near opera, Hofburg/Kunsthistorisches Museum, or City Hall) to its endpoint, the Beethovengang stop (despite what it says on the front of the tram, the Nussdorf stop isn't the end—stay on for one more stop). Exit the tram, cross the tracks, go uphill 40 yards, and look for

Drink with locals at a *Heuriger* wine garden.

Schübel-Auer Heuriger on your right. This is my favorite wine garden here. It offers a peaceful leafy garden and a rustic interior, and the buffet is big and user-friendly (opens at 16:00 Tue-Sat, 12:00 on Sun, closed Mon and generally Sun-Wed off-season, Kahlenberger Strasse 22, +43 1 370 2222). **Heuriger Kierlinger,** next door, is also good (opens at 15:30, closed most of August and periodically in off-season, Kahlenberger Strasse 20, +43 1 370 2264). **Mayer am Pfarrplatz** is a bustling place with photos of famous guests and elegant outdoor spaces (opens at 12:00, Pfarrplatz 2, +43 1 370 1287).

Ordering Food and Drink: In general, choose from the array of prepared items and hot dishes, pay at the buffet counter, and find a table. Then order (and pay for) your wine or other drinks from the waiter who will appear at your table. A quarter-liter (*Viertel*, FEER-tehl, 8 oz) glass of new wine costs about €2-3. *Most* (mohst) is lightly alcoholic grape juice—wine in its earliest stages, and usually available only in autumn. Once it gets a little more oomph, it's called *Sturm* (shtoorm), strictly a fall drink. Teetotalers can order *Traubenmost* (TROW-behn-mohst), grape juice.

Food is generally sold by weight, often in *"10 dag"* units (that's 100 grams, or about a quarter-pound). The buffet has several sections: The core of your meal is a warm dish, generally meat (such as ham, roast beef, roast chicken, roulade, or meatloaf). There are also warm sides (*Beilagen*), such as casseroles and sauerkraut, and a wide variety of cold salads and spreads. Many *Heuriger* staff speak English, and pointing also works.

OLD TOWN—NEAR ST. STEPHEN'S CATHEDRAL

These are all within a five-minute walk of the cathedral. U: Stephansplatz. (See the "Restaurants in Central Vienna" map.)

 $$$$ Labstelle My choice for a romantic meal, Bib Gourmand Michelin rating, nose-to-tail and farm-to-table ethic, enticing seasonal menu, lunch specials (closed Sun).

Lugeck 6, +43 1 236 2122, https://labstelle.at

$$$ Die Feinkosterei Schwarz-Hirsch Small-is-beautiful menu of Austrian food and wine, fine little plates for €8-12, fun way to experience top-quality traditional dishes family-style (daily).

Judenplatz 7, +43 1 396 1421, www.feinkosterei.wien

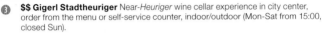 **$$ Gigerl Stadtheuriger** Near-*Heuriger* wine cellar experience in city center, order from the menu or self-service counter, indoor/outdoor (Mon-Sat from 15:00, closed Sun).

Just off Rauhensteingasse on Blumenstock, +43 1 513 4431

$ Trześniewski An institution, famous for elegant open-face finger sandwiches (22 options), small beers, point to whichever delights look tasty, pay and get drink tokens (Mon-Fri 8:30-19:30, Sat 9:00-18:00, closed Sun).

Dorotheergasse 2, +43 1 512 3291

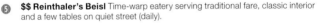 **$$ Reinthaler's Beisl** Time-warp eatery serving traditional fare, classic interior and a few tables on quiet street (daily).

Dorotheergasse 4, +43 1 513 1249

$$ Zwölf Apostelkeller ("Twelve Apostles Cellar") 500-year-old cellar, boisterous atmosphere with strolling musicians, cheap and accessible menu (daily).

Sonnenfelsgasse 3, +43 1 512 6777

OLD TOWN—NEAR AM HOF SQUARE

This square, just beyond the Graben, is surrounded by atmospheric medieval lanes with charming eateries. U: Herrengasse. (See the "Restaurants in Central Vienna" map.)

 $$ Venuss Vegan Bistro Bright, modern cafeteria promoting good vegan cooking, cold or hot buffet, fine outside seating (closed Sun).

Herrengasse 6, +43 1 890 8309

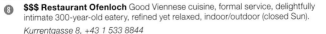 **$$$ Restaurant Ofenloch** Good Viennese cuisine, formal service, delightfully intimate 300-year-old eatery, refined yet relaxed, indoor/outdoor (closed Sun).

Kurrentgasse 8, +43 1 533 8844

⑨ $$ Brezel-Gwölb Tolkienesque nook, tight indoor tables, outdoor dining on quiet square, simple Viennese classics, unforgettable atmosphere, ideal for romantic late-night glass of wine, weekday lunch specials (daily).

Ledererhof 9, +43 1 533 8811

⑩ $ InterSpar (Groceries) am Schottentor Supermarket in fancy former Rothschild bank building, great deli section, cheap hot and cold meals to go, picnic in park across the Ring (Mon-Sat 8:00-20:00, closed Sun).

At Schottentor tram stop

OLD TOWN—NEAR THE OPERA

These eateries are within easy walking distance of the opera house. U: Karlsplatz. (See the "Restaurants in Central Vienna" map.)

⑪ $$$ Plachuttas Gasthaus zur Oper Proudly Austrian place, high-energy, specializes in local classics like *Tafelspitz* (boiled beef) and Wiener schnitzel (daily).

Walfischgasse 5, +43 1 512 2251

⑫ $$ Kurkonditorei Oberlaa Top choice among Viennese pastry connoisseurs, light meals, salads, vegetarian dishes, outdoor seating on Neuer Markt, more temptations and good seating upstairs (daily 8:00-20:00).

Neuer Markt 16, +43 1 5132 9360

⑬ $$ Le Bol Patisserie Bistro Modern place with old-school French vibe, fine salads, baguette sandwiches, fresh croissants, small terrace outside, cozy bistro inside, French-speaking staff (long hours daily).

Neuer Markt 14, +43 699 1030 1899

⑭ $$$ Danieli Ristorante Classy Italian, white-tablecloth dressy but not stuffy, reasonable prices, air-con in back room, outdoor seating (daily).

Opposite Neuer Markt at Himmelpfortgasse 3, +43 1 513 7913

⑮ Billa Corso Three floors of food, ready-made meals, eat inside (air-con) or on the square, great deli selection for lunch or picnic (daily 8:00-20:00).

Neuer Markt 17, corner of Seilergasse and Neuer Markt, +43 1 961 2133

EATING

MUSEUM DISTRICT—SPITTELBERG

Charming cobbled grid of traffic-free lanes and tables tumbling down sidewalks and into breezy courtyards; handy for Mariahilfer Strasse hotels; browse Spittelberggasse, Gutenberggasse, and Schrankgasse; great in summer, dead in bad weather. U3: Volkstheater/Museumsplatz. (See the "Restaurants Near Mariahilfer Strasse" map.)

 $$ Amerlingbeisl Charming place with casual atmosphere, seating on cobbled street or vine-covered courtyard, great value, mix of traditional Austrian and international dishes (daily).

Stiftgasse 8, +43 1 526 1660

 $$$ Zu Ebener Erde und Erster Stock Mostly traditional Austrian menu, signature is *Tafelspitz* (boiled beef), cute 18th-century building, casual and woody downstairs, fancy upstairs, al fresco tables along quiet street, seasonal specials (last seating at 20:30, closed Sat-Sun).

Burggasse 13, +43 1 523 6254, www.zu-ebener-erde-und-erster-stock.at

18 **$$ Glacis Beisl** Popular with locals, gravelly wine garden, outdoor tables appealing on a balmy evening, weekday lunch specials (daily until late).

Breitegasse 4, +43 1 526 5660, www.glacisbeisl.at

MARIAHILFER STRASSE AND THE NASCHMARKT

In this area you'll find reasonable cafés serving all types of cuisine. A short walk away are Spittelberg (see above) and the Naschmarkt. U: Neubaugasse or Zieglergasse. (See "Restaurants Near Mariahilfer Strasse" map.)

19 **$$ Trześniewski** The place for a quick yet traditional bite, same sandwiches as old town restaurant, minus the ambience (Mon-Fri 8:30-19:30, Sat 9:00-18:00, closed Sun).

Mariahilfer Strasse 95

20 **$ Schnitzelwirt** Old classic with 1950s patina, huge schnitzel (closed Sun).

Neubaugasse 52, +43 1 523 3771

 Billa Plus Supermarket for picnic fixings in basement of Gerngross shopping mall (Mon-Fri until 20:00, Sat until 18:00, closed Sun).

Mariahilfer Strasse 42

 **$-$$ Naschmarkt** Sprawling produce market good for a trendy dinner or gathering a picnic, thriving Old World scene, cafés, kebab and sausage stands (market open Mon-Fri 6:00-19:30, Sat until 18:00, closed Sun, closes earlier in winter; restaurants open later).

Between Linke Wienzeile and Rechte Wienzeile

Restaurants in Central Vienna

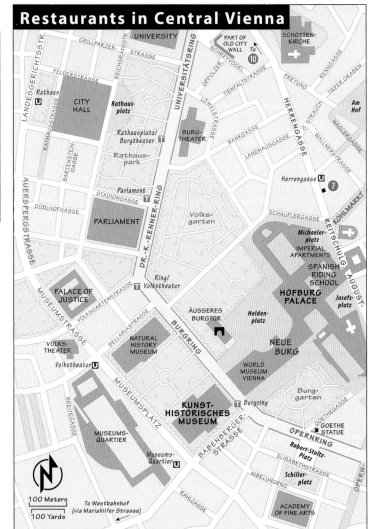

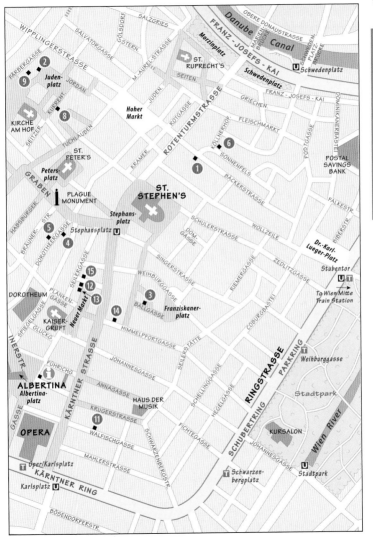

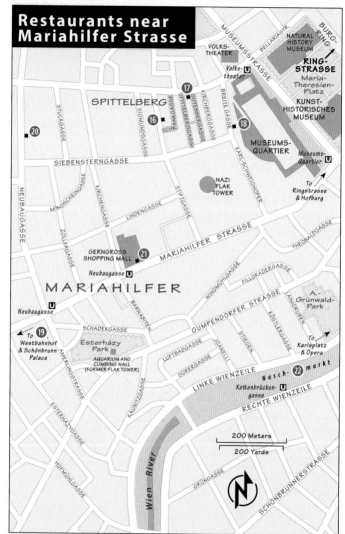

Restaurants near Mariahilfer Strasse

MUSEUMSSTRASSE

BELLARIAGTR.

BURG- RING

NATURAL HISTORY MUSEUM

VOLKS- THEATER

Volks- U *theater*

RING- STRASSE

Maria- Theresien- Platz

SPITTELBERG

17

16

GUTENBERGGASSE

KIRCHBERGGASSE

SPITTELBERGGASSE

BREITE GASSE

SCHRANKGASSE

SIGMUNDSGASSE

SCHMELZGASSE

KUNST- HISTORISCHES MUSEUM

18

MUSEUMS- QUARTIER

Museums- *Quartier* U

STUCKGASSE

20

SIEBENSTERNGASSE

NEUBAUGASSE

MONDSCHEINGASSE

KIRCHENGASSE

LINDENGASSE

STIFTGASSE

KARL-SCHWEIGHOFER

NAZI FLAK TOWER

To *Ringstrasse* *& Hofburg*

THEOBALDGASSE

ZOLLERGASSE

GERNGROSS SHOPPING MALL

21

MARIAHILFER STRASSE

Neubaugasse U

MARIAHILFER

WINDMÜHLGASSE

FILLGRADERGASSE

Neubaugasse U

BARNABITEN

GUMPENDORFER STRASSE

KÖSTLERGASSE

RAMGRUBEN

A.- Grünwald- Park

To *Westbahnhof* *& Schönbrunn* *Palace*

19

SCHADEKGASSE

Esterházy Park

AQUARIUM AND CLIMBING WALL (FORMER FLAK TOWER)

AMERLINGSTRASSE

LUFTBADGASSE

DÜRERGASSE

JOANELLI

STIEGEN

To *Karlsplatz* *& Opera*

ESTERHÁZYGASSE

KAUNITZGASSE

LINKE WIENZEILE

Nasch- markt

22

Kettenbrücken- U *gasse*

RECHTE WIENZEILE

HOFMÜHLGASSE

200 Meters

200 Yards

Wien River

GRUNGASSE

SCHÖNBRUNNERSTRASSE

Practicalities

HELPFUL HINTS

Travel Tips

Travel Advisories: Before traveling, check updated health and safety conditions, including restrictions for your destination, at Travel.State.gov (US State Department travel pages) and CDC.gov (Centers for Disease Control and Prevention).

Tourist Information: Vienna's main TI is behind the Vienna State Opera at Albertinaplatz (daily 9:00-18:00, theater box office, +43 1 24 553, www.vienna.info). There's also a TI at the airport (daily 9:00-18:00). The main TI's theater box office has all the options, knowledgeable salespeople, and information about the various venues.

Hurdling the Language Barrier: Most Viennese, especially those in the tourist trade, speak at least some English. Still, you'll get more smiles by using a few German pleasantries. It's polite to greet your fellow travelers in the hotel breakfast room in the morning (*Guten Morgen*) and greet shop owners as you enter (*Grüss Gott*). The Austrian form of German isn't much different from the Deutsch spoken by Germans—but those small differences are a big deal to Austrians. For example, the German *Guten Tag* sounds oddly uptight to Austrians, who prefer *Grüss Gott*—literally "May God greet you." Tacking an "*-l*" or "*-erl*" on the end of a word makes it a diminutive form—like adding "-ette" or "-ie" to an English word. Austrians appreciate any effort on your part to speak German, even if it's just *ein Bissl* (a little bit). To learn a few more German phrases, see page 197.

Time Zones: Austria is six/nine hours ahead of the East/West Coasts of the US. For a handy time converter, use the world clock app on your phone or download one (see www.timeanddate.com).

Business Hours: Shops are open from about 9:00 until 18:00-20:00 on weekdays, but close earlier on Saturday and are almost always closed on Sunday. Most banks are open weekdays roughly from 8:00 until 15:00.

Watt's Up: Europe's electrical system is 220 volts, instead of North America's 110 volts. Most electronics (laptops, phones, cameras) and appliances (hair dryers, CPAP machines) convert automatically, so you won't need a converter, but you will need an adapter plug with two round prongs, sold inexpensively at travel stores in the US.

Safety and Emergencies

Emergency and Medical Help: For any emergency service—ambulance, police, or fire—call 112 from a mobile phone or landline. If you get sick, do as the locals do and go to a pharmacist for advice. Or ask at your hotel for help—they'll know the nearest medical and emergency services.

Theft or Loss: The city has more than its share of pickpockets—especially in the train station, on trams, in and near crowded museums, and at places of drunkenness. Keep your passport and backup cash and cards in a money belt.

To replace a **passport,** you'll need to go in person to the US embassy (Boltzmanngasse 16, +43 1 313 390, http://at.usembassy.gov). If your credit and debit cards disappear, cancel and replace them, and report the loss immediately (call these 24-hour US numbers: Visa—+1 303 967 1096, Mastercard—+1 636 722 7111, and American Express—+1 336 393 1111). For more information, see RickSteves.com/help.

Drinking Water: The Viennese are proud of their perfectly drinkable tap water from alpine springs. You'll spot locals refilling their little bottles at fountains all over town. The city has installed public water fountains with signs reminding people to stay hydrated.

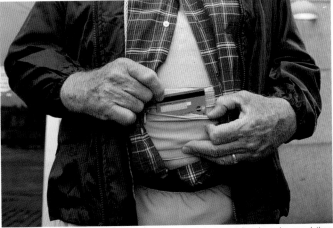

Use a money belt for large amounts of cash, credit cards, and passport. It tucks under your clothes.

PRACTICALITIES

Around Town

English Bookstore: Stop by the cool **Shakespeare & Co.,** in the historic and atmospheric Ruprechtsviertel district near the Danube Canal (Mon-Sat 9:00-21:00, closed Sun, north of Hoher Markt at Sterngasse 2, +43 1 535 5053, www.shakespeare.co.at). The biggest bookstore with a good English selection is **Morawa** (near the cathedral at Wollzeile 11). For locations, see the "Vienna's City Center" map on page 124.

Travel Agency: Conveniently located on Stephansplatz, **Ruefa** sells tickets for flights and trains (Mon-Fri 9:00-18:30, closed Sat-Sun, Stephansplatz 10—see "Vienna's City Center" map on page 124, +43 1 513 4524, Sandra speaks English).

ARRIVAL IN VIENNA

Vienna International Airport

Vienna's airport is 12 miles from the center and easy to reach from downtown (code: VIE, www.viennaairport.com). The arrivals hall has an array of services: TI, shops, ATMs, eateries, and a handy supermarket. Ramps lead down to the lower-level train station.

To get between the airport and central Vienna, you have three options:

By Train: Trains connect the airport with the Wien-Mitte Bahnhof, on the east side of the Ring. Choose between two ways of getting to Wien-Mitte: the regular S-7 S-Bahn train (€4.30, 24 minutes) and the express CAT train (€12, 16 minutes). Both run twice an hour on the same tracks. It's hard to justify spending almost €8 more to save eight minutes of time on the CAT. I'd take the S-7, unless the CAT is departing first and you're in a big hurry. Trains from downtown start running about 5:00, while the last train from the airport leaves about 23:30.

To take the **S-Bahn,** from the arrivals hall, go down either of the big ramps, follow the red ÖBB signs, then buy a regular two-zone public transport ticket from the red ticket machines. It's easiest to just type in your final destination and let the machine do the work. The price includes transfers to other trams, city buses, and S- and U-Bahn lines (see www.wienerlinien.at). Be aware that the Wien-Mitte Bahnhof U-Bahn station is called "Landstrasse." ÖBB Railjet trains

Helpful Websites

Vienna Tourist Information: Vienna.info
Austria Tourist Information: Austria.info
Passports and Red Tape: Travel.State.gov
Flights: Google Flights (international flights, www.google.com/travel/flights), SkyScanner.com (flights within Europe)
Airplane Carry-on Restrictions: TSA.gov
Train Schedules: Bahn.com
General Travel Tips: RickSteves.com (train travel, rail passes, car rental, travel insurance, packing lists, and more)

also run from the airport to Vienna's Hauptbahnhof (to connect to U-1) and to Wien Meidling (to connect to U-6).

To take the **CAT,** follow the green signage down the ramp to your right as you come out into the arrivals hall and buy a ticket from the green machines.

By Bus: Convenient express airport buses go to various points in Vienna, including Morzinplatz/Schwedenplatz U-Bahn station (for city-center hotels, 20 minutes) and Westbahnhof (for Mariahilfer Strasse hotels, 45 minutes). Double check your destination as you board (€9, round-trip-€15, 1/hour, buy ticket from driver, www.viennaairportlines.at).

By Taxi: The 30-minute ride into town costs a fixed €36 from the several companies with desks in the arrivals hall. You can also take a taxi from the taxi rank outside; you'll pay the metered rate (plus a trivial baggage surcharge), which should come out about the same.

Vienna's Train Stations

Vienna's huge **Hauptbahnhof** (central station) is just a few U-Bahn stops south of downtown. It has 12 pass-through tracks and all the services you may need.

To reach the city center from the Hauptbahnhof, including all my recommended hotels in the center, ride the U-1 (subway) for two to four stops (direction: Leopoldau) to Karlsplatz, Stephansplatz, or Schwedenplatz; ticket machines are near the escalators. You can also take tram #D (which runs along the Ring) from outside the

The Hauptbahnhof (main train station) is an easy U-Bahn, tram, or bus ride from the center.

main entrance. To reach Mariahilfer Strasse, ride U-1 three stops to Stephansplatz, then change to U-3 (direction: Ottaring), or hop on bus #13A. Tram #O runs from the station to Landstrasse and the Wien-Mitte station (for airport trains).

The **Westbahnhof** station (at the west end of Mariahilfer Strasse, on the U-3 and U-6 lines) has a bright, user-friendly mall of services, shops, and eateries. For the city center, follow orange signs to the U-3 (direction: Simmering). If your hotel is along Mariahilfer Strasse, your stop is on this line, but it may be simpler to walk. The small **Franz-Josefs-Bahnhof** station in the northern part of the city serves Krems and other points on the north bank of the Danube. There's no U-Bahn stop at the station, but convenient tram #D connects it to the city center.

Wien-Mitte Bahnhof, just east of the Ring, is the terminus for CAT and S-Bahn (suburban trains) to the airport (its U-Bahn station is called "Landstrasse").

GETTING AROUND VIENNA

By Public Transportation

Vienna's efficient transit system, operated by **Wiener Linien** (www.wienerlinien.at), includes trams, buses, U-Bahn (subway), and S-Bahn (faster suburban trains). It's fast, clean, and easy to navigate.

Stick to the tram to zip around the Ring (trams #1, #2, #71, #D, and #O) and take the U-Bahn to outlying sights and train stations. There are five color-coded U-Bahn lines: U-1 red, U-2 purple, U-3 orange, U-4 green, and U-6 brown. If you see a bus number that starts with N (such as #N38), it's a night bus, which operates after other public transit stops running.

Tickets and Passes: Trams, buses, and the U-Bahn and S-Bahn all use the same tickets (single tickets-€2.40, €2.60 on tram, good for one journey with necessary transfers). Buy tickets from vending machines, ticket offices in stations, or at some tobacco shops. Not all trams have ticket machines, so it's best to purchase tickets ahead of time. You cannot purchase tickets on buses.

Transit passes come in 24-hour (€8), 48-hour (€14.10), and 72-hour (€17.10) options. A seven-day *Wochenkarte* (€17.10) runs from Monday to Monday. The eight-day "Climate Ticket" (*Acht-Tage-Klimakarte,* €40.80) can be shared, making it a real saver for groups (but you must stay together).

Transit Tips: To get your bearings on buses, trams, the U-Bahn, and the S-Bahn, you'll want to know the end-of-the-line stop in the direction you're heading. For example, if you're in the city center at Stephansplatz and you want to take the U-Bahn to the main train station (Hauptbahnhof), you'd take U-1 going in the direction "Oberlaa." You must stamp your ticket at the barriers in U-Bahn and S-Bahn stations, and in the machines on trams and buses (stamp multiple-use passes only the first time you board). When purchasing tickets from vending machines, you can choose to have them validated before being printed. Cheaters pay a stiff fine (about €115).

On some trams, stop announcements are voice-only and easy to miss—carry a map and stay alert. Rookies miss stops because they fail to open the door. Push buttons, pull latches—do whatever it takes. Before you exit a U-Bahn station, study the wall-mounted street map and choose the most efficient exit.

Cute little electric buses wind through the tangled old center (from Schottentor to Stubentor). Bus #1A is best for a joyride—hop on and see where it takes you.

By Taxi or Uber

Though the city has a great public transit system and most of your time will be spent in the essentially traffic-free old town, you may need the occasional taxi. You can try waving one down, but locals either go to a taxi stand (there's generally one nearby) or call one. All Uber drivers in Vienna are also taxis—so, while Uber works here just like back home,

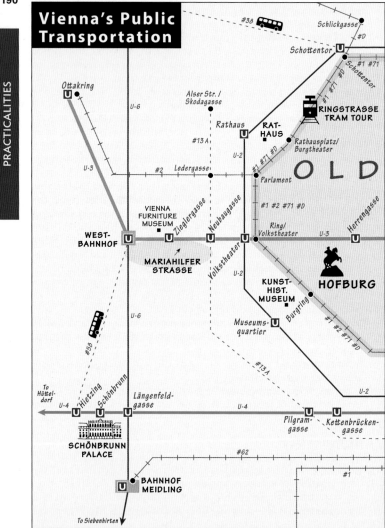

Vienna's Public Transportation

Ottakring

Alser Str. / Skodagasse

Rathaus

RAT-HAUS

#38

Schlickgasse

Schottentor

RINGSTRASSE TRAM TOUR

Rathausplatz/ Burgtheater

O L D

Parlament

Ledergasse

VIENNA FURNITURE MUSEUM

WEST-BAHNHOF

Zieglergasse

Neubaugasse

MARIAHILFER STRASSE

Ring/ Volkstheater

Herrengasse

Volkstheater

KUNST-HIST. MUSEUM

HOFBURG

Museums-quartier

Burgring

#58

To Hütteldorf

Hietzing

Schönbrunn

Längenfeld-gasse

Pilgram-gasse

Kettenbrücken-gasse

SCHÖNBRUNN PALACE

#62

BAHNHOF MEIDLING

To Siebenhirten

U-6
U-3
U-2
U-2
U-3
U-2
U-4
U-4
U-6
U-2

#13 A
#2
#13 A
#1 #2 #71 #D
#1 #71 #D
#1 #71 #D
#1 #2 #71 #D
#1
#D
#1 #71
#1 #2 #71 #D
#1

Schottentor

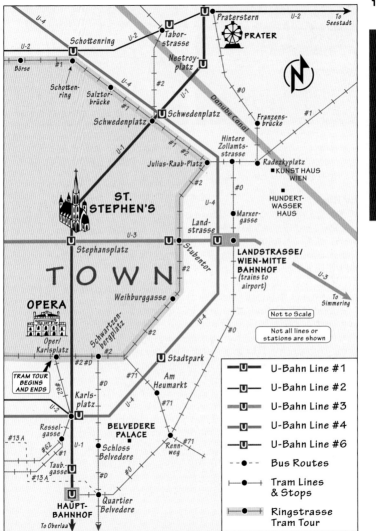

Vienna's U-Bahn (subway) is easy to use.

Use trams to expand your sightseeing.

it's essentially a taxi call service. Uber rates are a bit cheaper than official taxi metered rates, and there's no extra charge for the call.

By Bike

With more than 600 miles of bike lanes, Vienna is a great city on two wheels. The bike path along the Ring (following my Ringstrasse Tram audio tour) is wonderfully entertaining. Or ride along the Danube Canal, across Danube Island, and out to the modern Donau City business district. These routes are easy to follow on the *Radkarte* bike map available from the TI. Bike lanes are usually marked with red-colored pavement, but some are marked just with white lines.

WienMobil Rad (operated by Nextbike) has an app that lets you borrow bikes from public racks all over town. Before your trip, download the WienMobil Rad app and register with your credit card. To borrow a bike at a stand, open the app and enter the number of the bike you want; you'll receive a code to unlock it (€0.60/30 minutes, €14.90/24 hours, +43 1 790 9100, www.wienerlinien.at/wienmobil-app).

Pedal Power rents better-quality bikes (€6/hour, €19/4 hours, €30/24 hours, RS%—10 percent with this book, e-bikes available, daily May-Sept 9:00-18:00, shorter hours March-April and Oct-Nov, rental office near the opera house, a block beyond the Ring, at Bösendorferstrasse 5—see "Vienna's City Center" map on page 124, +43 1 729 7234, www.pedalpower.at).

Tipping

Tipping in Austria isn't as automatic and generous as it is in the US, but some general guidelines apply.

Restaurants: You don't need to tip if you order your food at a counter. Restaurants that have wait staff generally include a service charge in the bill, but it's common to tip by rounding up (about 5-10 percent). If paying with a credit card, be prepared to tip separately with cash or coins; credit card receipts often don't have a tip line.

Taxis: For a typical ride, round up your fare a bit (for instance, if the fare is €4.50, pay €5).

Services: For local guides, private drivers, or others who spend several hours with you, and significantly improve the quality of your trip, a healthy tip (of around 10 percent) is not extravagant. In general, if someone in the tourism or service industry does a super job for you, a small tip of a euro or two is appropriate. If you're not sure whether (or how much) to tip, ask a local for advice.

MONEY

Austria uses the euro currency: 1 euro (€) = about $1.10. To convert prices in euros to dollars add about 10 percent: €20 = about $22, €50 = about $55. Check Oanda.com for the latest exchange rates.

You'll use your **credit card** for purchases both big (hotels, advance tickets) and small (little shops, food stands). A "tap-to-pay" or "contactless" card is widely accepted and simple to use. Check to see if you already have—or can get—a tap-to-pay version of your credit card (look on the card for the tap-to-pay symbol—four curvy lines). Make sure you know the numeric four-digit PIN for each of your cards, both debit and credit. Request it if you don't have one, as it may be required for some purchases.

Use a **debit card** at ATMs (in Austria ask for a *Geldautomat*) to withdraw a small amount of local cash. While many transactions are by card these days, cash can help you out of a jam if your card randomly doesn't work, and can be useful to pay for things like tips and local guides. Keep backup cards and cash safe in a **money belt.**

At self-service payment machines (such as transit-ticket kiosks),

US cards may not work. In this case, look for a cashier who can process your card manually—or pay in cash.

STAYING CONNECTED

Making International Calls

From a Mobile Phone: Phone numbers in this book are presented exactly as you would dial them from a US mobile phone. For international access, press and hold 0 (zero) to get a + sign, then dial the country code (43 for Austria) and phone number.

From a US Landline to Europe: Replace + with 011 (US/Canada access code), then dial the country code (43 for Austria) and phone number.

From a European Landline to the US or Europe: Replace + with 00 (Europe access code), then dial the country code (43 for Austria, 1 for the US) and phone number. For more phoning help, see HowToCallAbroad.com.

Using Your Phone in Europe

Sign up for an international plan. To stay connected at a lower cost, sign up for an international service plan through your carrier. Most providers offer a simple bundle that includes calling, messaging, and data.

Use free Wi-Fi whenever possible. Unless you have an unlimited-data plan, save most of your online tasks for Wi-Fi. Most accommodations in Europe offer free Wi-Fi, and many cafés offer hotspots for customers. You may also find Wi-Fi at TIs, city squares, major museums, public-transit hubs, airports, and aboard trains and buses.

Save large-data tasks for Wi-Fi. If your included data is slow or metered, wait until you're on Wi-Fi to Skype or FaceTime, download apps, stream videos, or do other megabyte-greedy tasks. Using a navigation app such as Google Maps over a cellular network can require lots of data, so download maps when you're on Wi-Fi, then use the app offline.

Use Wi-Fi calling and messaging apps. Skype, FaceTime, and Google Meet are great for making free or low-cost calls or sending texts over Wi-Fi worldwide. WhatsApp is especially popular with

Use free Wi-Fi at your hotel to download apps, stream videos, and stay in touch.

Europeans, and is often the easiest way to communicate with guides, drivers, or other local contacts.

RESOURCES FROM RICK STEVES

Begin your trip at RickSteves.com: This book is just one of many in my series on European travel. I also produce a public television series, *Rick Steves' Europe,* and a public radio show, *Travel with Rick Steves.* My mobile-friendly website is the place to explore Europe in preparation for your trip. You'll find thousands of fun articles, beautiful photos, videos, and radio interviews; a wealth of money-saving tips; travel news dispatches; a video library of travel talks; our latest guidebook updates (RickSteves.com/update); and the free Rick Steves Audio Europe app with audio tours of Europe's top sights. You can also follow me on Facebook, Instagram, and Twitter.

Packing Checklist

Clothing

- [ ] 5 shirts: long- & short-sleeve
- [ ] 2 pairs pants (or skirts/capris)
- [ ] 1 pair shorts
- [ ] 5 pairs underwear & socks
- [ ] 1 pair walking shoes
- [ ] Sweater or warm layer
- [ ] Rainproof jacket with hood
- [ ] Tie, scarf, belt, and/or hat
- [ ] Swimsuit
- [ ] Sleepwear/loungewear

Money

- [ ] Debit card(s)
- [ ] Credit card(s)
- [ ] Hard cash (US $100-200)
- [ ] Money belt

Documents

- [ ] Passport
- [ ] Other required ID: Vaccine card, entry visa, etc.
- [ ] Driver's license, student ID, hostel card, etc.
- [ ] Tickets & confirmations: flights, hotels, trains, rail pass, car rental, sight entries
- [ ] Photocopies of important documents
- [ ] Insurance details
- [ ] Guidebooks & maps
- [ ] Extra passport photos
- [ ] Notepad & pen
- [ ] Journal

Toiletries

- [ ] Soap, shampoo, toothbrush, toothpaste, floss, deodorant, sunscreen, brush/comb, etc.
- [ ] Medicines & vitamins
- [ ] First-aid kit
- [ ] Glasses/contacts/sunglasses
- [ ] Face masks & hand sanitizer
- [ ] Sewing kit
- [ ] Packet of tissues (for WC)
- [ ] Earplugs

Electronics

- [ ] Mobile phone
- [ ] Camera & related gear
- [ ] Tablet/ebook reader/laptop
- [ ] Headphones/earbuds
- [ ] Chargers & batteries
- [ ] Plug adapters

Miscellaneous

- [ ] Day pack
- [ ] Sealable plastic baggies
- [ ] Laundry supplies
- [ ] Small umbrella
- [ ] Travel alarm/watch

Optional Extras

- [ ] Second pair of shoes
- [ ] Travel hairdryer
- [ ] Disinfecting wipes
- [ ] Water bottle
- [ ] Fold-up tote bag
- [ ] Small flashlight & binoculars
- [ ] Small towel or washcloth
- [ ] Tiny lock

German Survival Phrases

In the phonetics, ī sounds like the long i in "light," and bolded syllables are stressed.

Good day.	Grüss Gott.	**grews** gote
Do you speak English?	Sprechen Sie Englisch?	**shprehkh**-ehn zee **ehng**-lish
Yes. / No.	Ja. / Nein.	yah / nīn
I (don't) understand.	Ich verstehe (nicht).	ikh fehr-**shtay**-heh (nikht)
Please.	Bitte.	**bit**-teh
Thank you.	Danke.	**dahng**-keh
I'm sorry.	Es tut mir leid.	ehs toot meer līt
Excuse me.	Entschuldigung.	ehnt-**shool**-dig-oong
No problem.	Kein Problem.	kīn proh-**blaym**
Goodbye.	Auf Wiedersehen.	owf **vee**-der-zayn
How much is it?	Wieviel kostet das?	**vee**-feel **kohs**-teht dahs
Is it free?	Ist es umsonst?	ist ehs oom-**zohnst**
I'd like / We'd like...	Ich hätte gern / Wir hätten gern...	ikh **heh**-teh gehrn / veer **heh**-tehn gehrn
...a room.	...ein Zimmer.	īn **tsim**-mer
...a ticket to ____.	...eine Fahrkarte nach ____.	ī-neh **far**-kar-teh nahkh
Where is...?	Wo ist...?	voh ist
...the train station	...der Bahnhof	dehr **bahn**-hohf
...the bus station	...der Busbahnhof	dehr **boos**-bahn-hohf
...the tourist information office	...das Touristeninformationsbüro	dahs too-**ris**-tehn-in-for-maht-see-**ohns**-bew-roh
...the toilet	...die Toilette	dee toh-**leh**-teh
men / women	Herren / Damen	**hehr**-rehn / **dah**-mehn
left / right	links / rechts	links / rehkhts
straight	geradeaus	geh-**rah**-deh-ows
What time does this open / close?	Um wieviel Uhr wird hier geöffnet / geschlossen?	oom **vee**-feel oor veerd heer geh-**urf**-neht / geh-**shloh**-sehn
now / soon / later	jetzt / bald / später	yehtst / bahld / **shpay**-ter
today / tomorrow	heute / morgen	**hoy**-teh / **mor**-gehn

In a German/Austrian Restaurant

I'd like / We'd like...	Ich hätte gern / Wir hätten gern... ikh **heh**-teh gehrn / veer **heh**-tehn gehrn
...a reservation for...	...eine Reservierung für... ī-neh reh-zer-**feer**-oong fewr
...a table for one / two.	...einen Tisch für eine Person / zwei Personen. ī-nehn tish fewr ī-neh pehr-**zohn** / tsvī pehr-**zoh**-nehn
...the menu (in English), please.	...die Speisekarte (auf Englisch), bitte. dee **shpī**-zeh-kar-teh (owf **ehng**-lish) **bit**-teh
service (not) included	Trinkgeld (nicht) inklusive **trink**-gehlt (nikht) in-kloo-**zee**-veh
to go	zum Mitnehmen tsoom **mit**-nay-mehn
with / without	mit / ohne mit / **oh**-neh
and / or	und / oder oont / **oh**-der
menu (of the day)	(Tages-) Karte (**tah**-gehss-) **kar**-teh
specialty of the house	Spezialität des Hauses **shpayt**-see-ah-lee-**tayt** dehs **how**-zehs
appetizers	Vorspeise **for**-shpī-zeh
bread / cheese	Brot / Käse broht / **kay**-zeh
sandwich	Sandwich **zahnd**-vich
soup / salad	Suppe / Salat **zup**-peh / zah-**laht**
meat / poultry	Fleisch / Geflügel flīsh / geh-**flew**-gehl
fish / seafood	Fisch / Meeresfrüchte fish / **mee**-rehs-**froysh**-teh
fruit / vegetables	Obst / Gemüse ohpst / geh-**mew**-zeh
dessert	Nachspeise **nahkh**-shpī-zeh
coffee / tea	Kaffee / Tee kah-**fay** / tay
wine	Wein vīn
red / white	rot / weiß roht / vīs
glass / bottle	Glas / Flasche glahs / **flah**-sheh
beer	Bier beer
Cheers!	Prost! prohst
The bill, please.	Rechnung, bitte. **rehkh**-noong **bit**-teh
Delicious!	Lecker! **lehk**-er

INDEX

Start your trip at

Our website enhances this book and turns

Explore Europe

At ricksteves.com you can browse through thousands of articles, videos, photos and radio interviews, plus find a wealth of money-saving travel tips for planning your dream trip. And with our mobile-friendly website, you can easily access all this great travel information anywhere you go.

TV Shows

Preview the places you'll visit by watching entire half-hour episodes of *Rick Steves' Europe* (choose from all 100 shows) on-demand, for free.

ricksteves.com

your travel dreams into affordable reality

Radio Interviews

Enjoy ready access to Rick's vast library of radio interviews covering travel tips and cultural insights that relate specifically to your Europe travel plans.

Travel Forums

Learn, ask, share! Our online community of savvy travelers is a great resource for first-time travelers to Europe, as well as seasoned pros.

Travel News

Subscribe to our free Travel News e-newsletter, and get monthly updates from Rick on what's happening in Europe.

Classroom Europe®

Check out our free resource for educators with 500 short video clips from the *Rick Steves' Europe* TV show.

Audio Europe™

Rick's Free Travel App

Get your FREE Rick Steves Audio Europe™ app to enjoy…

- Dozens of self-guided tours of Europe's top museums, sights and historic walks
- Hundreds of tracks filled with cultural insights and sightseeing tips from Rick's radio interviews
- All organized into handy geographic playlists
- For Apple and Android

With Rick whispering in your ear, Europe gets even better.

Find out more at ricksteves.com

Pack Light and Right

Gear up for your next adventure at ricksteves.com

Light Luggage

Pack light and right with Rick Steves' affordable, custom-designed rolling carry-on bags, backpacks, day packs and shoulder bags.

Accessories

From packing cubes to moneybelts and beyond, Rick has personally selected the travel goodies that will help your trip go smoother.

Shop at ricksteves.com

Rick Steves has

Save time and energy

This guidebook is your independent-travel toolkit. But for all it delivers, it's still up to you to devote the time and energy it takes to manage the preparation and logistics that are essential for a happy trip. If that's a hassle, there's a solution.

Rick Steves Tours

A Rick Steves tour takes you to Europe's most interesting places with great guides and small groups.

great tours, too!

with minimum stress

We follow Rick's favorite itineraries, ride in comfy buses, stay in family-run hotels, and bring you intimately close to the Europe you've traveled so far to see. Most importantly, we take away the logistical headaches so you can focus on the fun.

Join the fun

This year we'll take thousands of free-spirited travelers—nearly half of them repeat customers—along with us on four dozen different itineraries, from Ireland to Italy to Athens. Is a Rick Steves tour the right fit for your travel dreams? Find out at ricksteves.com, where you can check seat availability and sign up.

Europe is best experienced with happy travel partners. We hope you can join us.

See our itineraries at ricksteves.com

A Guide for Every Trip

BEST OF GUIDES

Full-color guides in an easy-to-scan format, focusing on top sights and experiences in popular destinations

Best of England
Best of Europe
Best of France
Best of Germany

Best of Ireland
Best of Italy
Best of Scotland
Best of Spain

COMPREHENSIVE GUIDES

City, country, and regional guides printed on Bible-thin paper. Packed with detailed coverage for a multi-week trip exploring iconic sights and more

Amsterdam &
  the Netherlands
Barcelona
Belgium: Bruges, Brussels,
  Antwerp & Ghent
Berlin
Budapest
Central Europe
Croatia & Slovenia
England
Florence & Tuscany
France
Germany
Great Britain
Greece: Athens &
  the Peloponnese
Iceland

Ireland
Istanbul
Italy
London
Paris
Portugal
Prague & the Czech Republic
Provence & the French
  Riviera
Rome
Scandinavia
Scotland
Sicily
Spain
Switzerland
Venice
Vienna, Salzburg & Tirol

Many guides are available as ebooks.

POCKET GUIDES
Compact guides for shorter city trips

Amsterdam	Italy's Cinque Terre	Prague
Athens	London	Rome
Barcelona	Munich & Salzburg	Venice
Florence	Paris	Vienna

SNAPSHOT GUIDES
Focused single-destination coverage

Basque Country: Spain & France
Copenhagen & the Best of Denmark
Dublin
Dubrovnik
Edinburgh
Hill Towns of Central Italy
Krakow, Warsaw & Gdansk
Lisbon
Loire Valley
Madrid & Toledo
Milan & the Italian Lakes District
Naples & the Amalfi Coast
Nice & the French Riviera
Normandy
Northern Ireland
Norway
Reykjavík
Rothenburg & the Rhine
Sevilla, Granada & Southern Spain
St. Petersburg, Helsinki & Tallinn
Stockholm

CRUISE PORTS GUIDES
Reference for cruise ports of call

Mediterranean Cruise Ports
Scandinavian & Northern European
  Cruise Ports

TRAVEL SKILLS & CULTURE
Greater information and insight

Europe 101
Europe Through the Back Door
Europe's Top 100 Masterpieces
European Christmas
European Easter
European Festivals
For the Love of Europe
Italy for Food Lovers
Travel as a Political Act

PHRASE BOOKS & DICTIONARIES

French
French, Italian & German
German
Italian
Portuguese
Spanish

PLANNING MAPS

Britain, Ireland & London
Europe
France & Paris
Germany, Austria & Switzerland
Iceland
Ireland
Italy
Scotland
Spain & Portugal

PHOTO CREDITS

Avalon Travel
Hachette Book Group
1700 Fourth Street
Berkeley, CA 94710

Printed in China by RR Donnelley
Fourth Edition. First printing May 2024.

ISBN 978-1-64171-623-9

For the latest on Rick's talks, guidebooks, tours, public television series, and public radio show, contact Rick Steves' Europe, 130 Fourth Avenue North, Edmonds, WA 98020, +1 425 771 8303, RickSteves.com, rick@ricksteves.com.

Rick Steves' Europe

Managing Editor: Jennifer Madison Davis
Editorial Group Manager: Cathy Lu
Editors: Glenn Eriksen, Tom Griffin, Suzanne Kotz, Rosie Leutzinger, Teresa Nemeth, Jessica Shaw, Carrie Shepherd, Chelsea Wing
Researcher: Cary Walker
Creative Director: Sandra Hundacker
Maps & Graphics: Orin Dubrow, David C. Hoerlein, Lauren Mills, Mary Rostad

Avalon Travel

Senior Editor and Series Manager: Madhu Prasher
Associate Managing Editors: Jamie Andrade, Sierra Machado
Copy Editor: Kelly Lydick
Proofreader: Nikki Ioakimedes
Indexer: Claire Splan
Production & Typesetting: Christine DeLorenzo
Cover Design: Kimberly Glyder Design
Interior Design: Darren Alessi
Maps & Graphics: Kat Bennett

Let's Keep on Travelin'

Your trip doesn't need to end.

Follow Rick on social media!